LEE HUXLEY

GOD IS SEX, NOT SADISM

WHY THE SINNERS ARE THOSE WHO CONDEMN SEX, NOT THOSE WHO CELEBRATE IT

LEE HUXLEY

GOD IS SEX, NOT SADISM

WHY THE SINNERS ARE THOSE WHO CONDEMN SEX, NOT THOSE WHO CELEBRATE IT

MEREO
Cirencester

Mereo Books

1A The Wool Market Dyer Street Cirencester Gloucestershire GL7 2PR
An imprint of Memoirs Publishing www.mereobooks.com

God is sex, not sadism: 978-1-86151-593-3

First published in Great Britain in 2015
by Mereo Books, an imprint of Memoirs Publishing

The address for Memoirs Publishing Group Limited can be found at
www.memoirspublishing.com

The Memoirs Publishing Group Ltd Reg. No. 7834348

The Memoirs Publishing Group supports both The Forest Stewardship Council®
(FSC®) and the PEFC® leading international forest-certification organisations. Our
books carrying both the FSC label and the PEFC® and are printed on FSC®-certified
paper. FSC® is the only forest-certification scheme supported by the leading
environmental organisations including Greenpeace. Our paper procurement policy
can be found at www.memoirspublishing.com/environment

Typeset in 11/15ptPlantin
by Wiltshire Associates Publisher Services Ltd. Printed and bound in Great Britain
by Printondemand-Worldwide, Peterborough PE2 6XD

CONTENTS

Preface

Introduction

PREFACE

This is a book about art, dance, sex, the legalisation of prostitution, and *joie de vivre*. The last thing I want is to bore the reader with too much religion bashing. However, in order to sell the Tantric God of sexual love to the world, I have to explain why I feel we need a new model of God. Monotheism is arguably a major cause of most of the world's problems today and is well past its sell-by date. I postulate that if you get God wrong you get it all wrong, and monotheism has got God seriously wrong, as I hope to explain in due course.

This book is a prime example of radical rationalism. I was born in 1948, the year the state of Israel was fatefully established, laying the foundations of a new and dangerous geopolitical flashpoint with huge metaphysical implications, and this was after humanity had already disgraced itself with two heinous world wars. I am old enough to have lived through the psychological perils of what followed, namely the cold war and nuclear proliferation. The height of the cold war was the Cuban Missile Crisis of 1962, when the world came very close to suicidal megadeath simply through the stupidity of politicians. As the world now looks even more of a madhouse than it did in my youth, I might be excused for being a hardened cynic who is justified in regarding politics and religion as twin forces of necrotic spiritual dementia that are locked into a terrible dance of death that can only have a tragic ending for all of us unless there is a massive paradigm shift. Many academics write pretentious books about the need for a paradigm shift, but their ideas are never radical or far-reaching enough to make a difference. This is not the case with my book. This book throws away all the rules and dares to take logic and reason wherever it leads us, irrespective of the consequences.

Added to this, I have been diagnosed with prostate cancer, which seriously limits my time to impart to others what I think are sacred revolutionary ideas, and goes some way to explaining my urgency and extremism. President Obama in his last State of the Union speech said "Let's make America the country that cures cancer once and for all." He implied that to find a cure to this seemingly incurable mass killer is simply a matter of political will and resources. If this is true, why didn't America think of this before it wasted trillions of dollars in Vietnam, Iraq and Afghanistan? The crass mistakes of American foreign policy throughout my lifetime have not only helped to structure the doomsday machine we now live in but feels when confronted with the God he or she has formerly rejected. This is a book about tantric art, not Christian theology, so I'm not going to attempt to refute this risible excuse or any of the other pitiful examples of illogic and sophistry that most Christians use to cover up their deep unease about the hellfire doctrine. I have already refuted these in a book I published earlier entitled *Sex and the Devil's Wager,* which I strongly advise my readers to study in order to better understand my radical thesis. This revolutionary book exposes the problem of global hell-blindness and its dire consequences for all of us and proposes the unthinkable - that Jesus is not the Son of God but the Son of Evil. The threat of hell and the promise of paradise is the theological cornerstone of Islam and this horrible blasphemy is being used by ISIL today to brainwash children into becoming jihadists and suicide bombers. Hell is the burning issue of our times – it is not a non-issue as everyone seems to think.

But I would like to make one important point that I hope the reader will bear in mind at all times. Millions of Muslims and Christians today and throughout history agree with my position that Jesus himself believed in hell as a place of eternal physical torture for non-Christians. So the burden of proof lies with those who would like to exonerate Christ. Islam itself totally endorses the idea that Jesus believed in hell. But the real issue is this: why did Jesus not condemn the doctrine outright and emphatically? Many Jews of his time believed in hell. The Pharisees, for example, believed in hell and the concept of eternal torment was part of everyday theological discourse. So even if you could argue that Jesus didn't necessarily teach hell, you then have to explain why, if he is supposed to be a great prophet and a paragon of virtue, he didn't publicly and vociferously condemn this blasphemy against God. I know of no single record of Jesus Christ ever showing disapproval of hell and this, as far as I know, is true of all the gnostic and apocryphal scriptures. The only thing that would make any of the multiple 'versions' of Jesus acceptable to me, as a good and enlightened man, is if I was presented with clear evidence that he categorically condemned posthumous torture at the hands of God. A true prophet would have seen that this doctrine was the greatest blasphemy of his times and would have gone out of his way to distance himself from it.

Just what has happened to the doctrine of hell that used to be preached from every pulpit, unwittingly accusing God of being a cosmic sadist? Islamist terrorism has created such a climate of fear that genuine debate about religion has been gagged and any criticism of religion is now defined by the Christian state and the media as racism, hate speech or Islamophobia. I totally agree in principle with religious freedom, but I truly believe Judaism, Christianity and Islam are not authentic religions but superstitions.

I'm not just playing with words here in some kind of semantic grandstanding. I'm confident that I can defend this position against the academic establishment. Hinduism is far from perfect, which is why I'm not a Hindu, but at least Hinduism has great metaphysical insights that deepen our understanding of God. That is why I recognise it as a meaningful religion. But if you define a religion as a set of beliefs that facilitate understanding of God and the creation or the universe, then monotheism arguably does the opposite. A true religion would not teach that God is a cosmic sadist who tortures his creatures for all eternity in the next world – a God we are told by believers themselves (as I shall shortly demonstrate) who thinks it's a good thing to burn women alive in their trillions for all eternity without a second of respite from agony!

The default definition of monotheism in Western civilization is that whether God is true or not, its moral teachings are consistent with basic secular ideas of right and wrong and apologists cite the ten commandments or the story of the Good Samaritan for support. Unfortunately something quite shocking has been conveniently overlooked that makes a nonsense of uncritical religious freedom. My central argument is this: if it could be demonstrated that the idea of God tormenting his creatures in hell is the most evil idea ever imagined, and furthermore that this idea is taught in the Bible and the Koran, what justification would remain for tolerating religions that teach such ideas, ideas that totally conflict with secular concepts of human rights? Religious freedom is only part of the Declaration of Human Rights, because of its almost criminal failure to understand the full implications of the stealth evil that religion embodies in some of its doctrines.

This book attempts to persuade the reader that we have to change the default definition of monotheism, and especially Christianity and Islam. Once this is done the path is cleared for what some call the Age of Aquarius, but what I prefer to call the new and final Age of Reason and the arrival of Tantric paganism or Tantric Humanism in a world that desperately needs a spiritual blood transfusion.

Finally I would like the reader to understand where I'm coming from in terms of a personal lifelong struggle. From my teenage years I have been striving in all sorts of ways to get a public debate on hell. I have written to countless TV stations and organisations, published a book on the subject and challenged religious correspondents to justify their support for hellfire religion, and nothing I have done has led to any lessening in the sinister cultural silence about this vitally important issue which everyone apart from a few militant atheists sees as a non-issue.

This then for me is personal. I've devoted years of my life to it, and now I face premature death with no sign that any of my efforts have borne fruit. In the last chapter I explain why I think Amnesty International is a hypocritical organisation. I had a correspondence with them about what I feel is their failure to publicly condemn the religious doctrine of eternal torture. My point is simply one of intellectual consistency: if torture is wrong in this world, is it not wrong in the next?

INTRODUCTION

However hyperbolic my claim may sound to others, I am convinced my paintings have the most profound and revolutionary message in the history of art: they make the startling proclamation that God is sex. This bizarre and subversive phrase 'God is sex' may even strike some as a profanity. I would use the phrase 'God is Love' if it hadn't been ruined by Christianity. In Christianity this phrase arguably means self-serving charity and love for a sado-God who disapproves of any kind of human sexuality that is not intended for procreation using the missionary position.

My art is based in Tantra, which I am happy to define as an erotic non-doctrinal religion. Tantra uses the sexual act as a metaphor for God. Hopefully this erotic worldview will be explained more fully in the following pages. Because Judaism, Christianity and Islam are arguably anti-erotic, it is these religions that Tantra (or at least my brand of Tantra) implicitly opposes and defines as Armageddon death cults. My erotic art, which focuses to a large extent on the nude form, and my passion for sex with prostitutes will not endear me to most feminists. Nevertheless, at risk of vexing my female readers, I claim that feminism, despite its obvious achievements, is now failing women, largely because it has ignored some of the unique insights of Tantra. I believe I can offer a new feminist paradigm for the future and I draw support for my thesis from Mary Daly, a seminal Catholic, feminist theologian who before her death, self-identified with paganism and denounced most of the feminist critique of religion as a failure to alert women to its hidden evils. My art therefore, from the vantage point of lateral thinking, is devoted to the liberation of women, and hopefully a new sexual revolution that will enable women finally to achieve, not just sexual equality but possibly better sex! However far-fetched this claim might appear at first, I will endeavour to vindicate it in due course.

I believe that not just UK society but global society is sex-phobic. Many societies are multi-faith cultures and most faiths are highly moralistic in sexual matters. Even atheistic communist countries like China and the old Soviet Union stem from Marxist ideology, and neither Karl Marx nor Chairman Mao are exactly noted for their liberal views about human sexuality. Both China and India have potent erotic cultural traditions which they have arguably turned their backs on, as if they are now ashamed of their wonderful Tantric legacies.

Is my obsession with feminine beauty unhealthy? I love

being a sexual zealot, but this arguably makes me a sexual outlaw, incurring the puritanical disapproval of society. One reason for my beautiful addiction is that it is my way of protesting at centuries of irrational body phobia. In our present social climate, engineered by the strange convergence of certain anti-erotic feminist narratives and religious conventions, the idea of celebrating sex and the sexual organs in art and sacred ritual is not viewed with enthusiasm. The message of my art is a wake-up call. It says, it's time to grow up! It is time in the twenty-first century to overcome our deep fear of genital imagery. Why? Because it is illogical and arguably an insult to God, according to Tantra.

My thesis will not be well received by most feminists, who argue, falsely in my view, that to isolate body parts like the vulva is automatically to reduce women to those body parts. In past pagan cultures this body phobia was far less prevalent and sometimes sex, procreation and the human genitals were openly celebrated in temple art and religion. The human genitals are the most potent markers of the elemental gender forces and the specific instruments of procreation, and therefore in Tantra represent the life force. Surely they need to be honoured, not stigmatised and feared as shameful and dangerous to children, as they are in our own times?

Some objectors to this line of thought do not even accept the elemental binary of male and female, and any attempt to celebrate heterosexual procreation is likely to raise objections from the gay and transgender communities. Despite the complexity of this issue I firmly believe it is more valid than ever before to celebrate human sexuality, according to the Tantric principles I embrace in my art. I don't believe procreative sex has ever been properly celebrated because, in pagan times, they had the rituals and the temples but they didn't have the science, and in our own times we've got the science but not the rituals and the temples!

I find the issue of gender reassignment perplexing, depressing and messy, and I have to admit, aesthetically scary. The Asians carry it off much better than anyone else, but reassignment surgery, has produced some very strange-looking people in the West. Perhaps my concerns have been influenced by the fact that I caught gonorrhoea from a ladyboy who fooled me into accepting oral sex in Thailand, and on another occasion I had to throw a transsexual out of my hotel after I'd examined his vagina (thankfully before penetration) and found it to be pure fakery. Some would say that because of gay sex and transsexuality, the conventional binary of male and female heterosexuality should be denied any kind of primacy. I disagree and say that the impact undermining the primacy of heterosexuality from gays and transsexuals is even more reason to celebrate the heterosexual procreative principle which for the whole of human evolution has nobly populated the world with generations that unfolded through the millennia with the regularity of a heartbeat. Is it not time to build temples to honour this sacred puissance from the *yoni* and the *lingam*?

I hope to demonstrate that what I call 'anti-erotic feminism', or feminism opposed to prostitution and soft porn, is now in alliance with the ideologues of monotheistic body phobia and shares common goals in preventing a revival of pagan, sex-positive values. How is it possible that in Western 'civilization' it is considered totally unacceptable for children to be exposed to images of the greatest ongoing event in human life, namely the sexual act – to which they owe their very existence, yet they can be freely indoctrinated on an industrial scale with evil superstitions that contradict science, reason and moral decency? Allowing children to be exposed to images of the sexual organs that created them is obscene, according to prevailing mores, but feeding them a religion that tells them there is a real-life hell and they will go there if they dare to have sex before marriage is laudable! Such indoctrination is endorsed by the law, academia, the mass media and politicians, all trumpeting the marvels of religious freedom and the rights of religious parents and state educators to force their anti-scientific beliefs on hapless youngsters. Faith schools in my opinion are a form of child abuse. Truly, to a man like me who has Tantric wisdom, the world is a loony bin of moral schizophrenia.

My religion, which is syncretistic and rationalistic, is only based in Tantra. Tantra is not a rigid revealed doctrine like Christianity and Islam. In essence it is subversive and individualistic and you are free to use whatever works for you and reject what doesn't. It derives from esoteric Hindu and Buddhist metaphysics, and is also the major inspiration behind my erotic art. Tantra reversed many of the orthodox values of Hinduism and Buddhism and is naturally anarchistic and blissfully hedonistic and life-positive. For this reason, as I say, it perfectly lends itself to personal interpretation.

My Tantra is my own, and that's how it should be. Your

religion should be a personal relationship with the universe and God. Organised religion is just insidious mass thought control which trains people to think in a box. I take from Tantra what I need, which is a few keynote concepts, the first being that God is sex and therefore that sex is divine. The second is that dance and prostitution are sacraments and should be quintessential elements in modern civilization. Thirdly, I embrace with passion the Tantric reverence for the human body as a microcosm of the universe. Tantra argues that if the human body is arguably God's supreme masterpiece, it is literally blasphemous to make the genitals victims of shame and gratuitous censorship. Last but not least, Tantra teaches that sex is a way of power or self-empowerment. If sex is the life force, then in Tantra's mythopoetic worldview, he or she who understands this life force and can channel it can eventually achieve supernormal powers.

Personally, I have no use for esoteric rituals or the much-publicised commercial Tantric techniques for improving your sex life or reinvigorating a failing marriage. This Americanised populist Tantra is for me tame and less important than its lesser-known transgressive world-changing elements. This kind of Tantra is like yoga stripped of its spiritual heritage, but worse, because Tantra is subversive and the world needs subversion more than meditation. Tantra which has been emasculated in order to be acceptable to Christian America is not for me. Real Tantra is militant sexual radicalism aimed at freeing the world from Thanatos and erotic delusions based on monotheistic body phobia.

My work, like Tantra, is a celebration of sex and the

human body, especially the feminine form, which for me is the summit of visual experience. In Tantra, God is literally sex in the sense that the Godhead, or Ultimate Reality, is conceived of as a god and goddess making love in the form of the *yab-yum*. The yab-yum, which is one of the most iconic motifs in Tantric art, is often actualised in the form of a bronze or copper figurine. The creative and procreative energy of humanity and the universe is therefore mythopoetically defined as God - the divine cosmic life force. In Tantra the universe is created through ecstatic dance and lovemaking. The cosmos emerges from the yoni-cunt of the Goddess, but every particle is suffused with the pain of primal separation and the desire to return to its original oneness. In Tantra, every time humans make love they are re-enacting the primordial cosmic sex act between Shiva and Shakti. The Absolute is genderless but at some point experiences desire for a male/female dynamic and manifests itself as the androgynous god Ardhanari, who has a male and female body combined in one cosmic deity. This god then divides into the yab-yum as a couple, Shiva and Shakti, joined in sexual bliss. The Absolute divides itself into male and female in order to love, dance and procreate. Perhaps divine perfection is a paradox because it cannot experience desire: perhaps it lacks the dynamic of sex and evolution and needs to create an 'Other': a gender binary. Whatever the reason, the fact remains that according to this Tantric mythology, God and the universe are driven by desire – Eros - the love of life.

This is what religion in the future should really be about without monotheism poisoning the waters of the world soul: everybody has their own storytime. God's existence is arguably a given. God is a datum and a factual synonym for Truth or the ineffable Absolute. Everything else is storytime – mythopoetic pragmatism which is best exemplified by Hindu and Greek mythology. Greek and Hindu mythology may not be objectively true but it gives us important insights into human psychology, our spiritual needs and our cogitations about God. Mythology actually imparts insights about different concepts and models of God and enriches our lives as long as we never forget it is storytime – but a deeply meaningful narrative nevertheless. Christians and Muslims take their mythology literally which is why they are still laughably waiting for Jesus to return! My storytime is the yab-yum. It may not be objectively true but it is subjectively true and facilitates self-understanding and my relationship to the Absolute.

When I first learned about this myth, whereby God becomes Shiva and Shakti separated, yet yearning to return to primal unity, it was a personal epiphany because it perfectly explained my own addiction. I knew it wasn't scientifically true but it 'felt' more authentic and real to me than anything else. For me it was subjectively true that I was Shiva continually searching for my other half, namely Shakti. However in my personal pagan pantheon, Aphrodite, goddess of sexual love, and Kwan Yin, goddess of love and mercy, play a major role. Aphrodite is the patroness of prostitutes and symbolises the *feminine* principle or feminine beauty. Shakti on the other hand is the *female* principle, which embodies all women whether young or old, beautiful or ugly. Aphrodite, the Greek goddess of love, is, like all goddesses, an aspect or avatar of Shakti, and is the feminine principle within her. On the other hand Kali is the warrior aspect of Shakti and dances, we are told, naked or 'space clad'.

Each man is entitled to define the feminine principle for himself as the sum total of all the women he personally finds desirable. What constitutes femininity for women, be they lesbian or not, is up to them, but for me a feminine woman is a woman I want to make love to. Aphrodite is my cosmic lover and is often represented in my paintings alongside images of my girls. Just as Aphrodite is an avatar of the mother goddess Shakti, so my girls are avatars of Aphrodite. She is the embodiment of every woman who is desirable to me, past, present and future. When I make love to a bar girl I am having sex with Aphrodite.

When I understood these Tantric insights I knew I could never love a single woman in the conventional sense of the word, because no matter how much I loved any individual woman I would always be yearning for others – for other avatars of Aphrodite. All beautiful women are the same woman to me, and I feel bonded to them because they are all permutations of my 'cosmic wife'. It actually upsets me every time a beautiful woman ignores me and passes me by without feeling the slightest trace of the yearning I feel for her. In my Freudian id I feel rejected and snubbed by beautiful women who don't instantly greet me like a lover and take me home with them to make love. I feel I know them already, but I'm burning with curiosity to see them naked and to appreciate their magical anatomical uniqueness compared to the others I've already documented. They may see me simply as an anonymous face in the crowd, but I recognise them as my cosmic spouse. Only when I have made love to every one of her myriad parts will I have actually possessed Aphrodite herself.

I know this ambition is impossible to achieve in a thousand lifetimes, but this does not stop my craving to possess her. In the last few years I have had sex with over five hundred sex workers, and yet I feel I have only taken the first tentative steps of my quest for the Holy Grail that will only be unjustly terminated by death. This is why the yab-yum is such a powerful and exciting icon to me, because it gives sex the highest possible importance by making God a metaphor for sex: God is sex, and from this I conclude that for me, sex is God – sex is Divine.

Am I oversexed? Not at all. My libido is galvanised and driven by my eyes and the loftiest sentiments and not by any animalistic scrotal frenzy. It is as much about seeing as it is about fucking. I am intoxicated with the feminine body as God's masterpiece – God's aesthetic magnum opus.

When in my early fifties my last serious relationship came to an acrimonious end, I felt washed up and too old and penurious ever to achieve sex with a beautiful woman again before I shuffled off this mortal coil. I wasn't looking for love, because I'd had enough of long-term relationships with all the stresses and strains that often come from cohabiting with partners in relative poverty, which was always the case with me. In my last years on Earth I wanted sex and physical beauty more than the social company of women.

I had by this time experimented with a few 'in-call' prostitutes, but these experiences had been disappointing because they involved visiting a prostitute contacted through a phone box card and turning up for a blind date at a grubby location for half an hour of deeply unsatisfying sex. I knew I was just on a conveyor belt and the next guy was often waiting outside for me to finish. The only time I ever failed to get an erection was on one of these occasions, and the sex worker turned out to be a very big lady who turned off my libido like a water tap when she undressed. It was only much later when I owned a laptop and could get a better deal with home visits from escorts that my sex life picked up a little.

In my late fifties I joined a Ukrainian marriage agency, out of curiosity more than anything else. I was not looking for love per se, but something deep inside me still needed the attention of beautiful women. I craved their respect and affection, and even though the feedback I got from an assortment of cyber babes was artificial, it was still better than nothing and brought me comfort. My libido was set on fire every night for months and months as I chatted with these Eastern European glamour girls, and I even visited one of them, in Poltava, just to find out if the goddess was real. But all this sloppy romance ended in disaster. The full story of my experiences in the Ukraine and then Asia are documented in more detail in my last book *I Took the Sex Gods to Thailand*. I hope my readers will make it their intention to read this true story, which shows a completely different side to prostitution from the killjoy establishment narrative.

My life changed dramatically after the Ukraine fiasco when a friend of mine invited me to Hong Kong, where he said I could find many beautiful women in the bars. In Asia, he said, prostitution was more customer friendly and had an exotic festive flavour you couldn't get in the West. I didn't believe him at first, but I decided to put his boast to the test, because I had nothing to lose from trying. Imagine my surprise when I found out he was right. As soon as I got to Hong Kong I felt the vibe: unlike London, it had a palpable sexual energy. On my first night I walked into a bar called Neptune with my friend Spike, and my life changed dramatically. In that life-defining moment I felt I became truly reborn as Shiva. The bar was heaving with oriental women from all over Asia, and they were all available! This was what I had been looking for all my life and had never been able to find in my miserable Christian homeland, where sleazy, sordid Soho and lapdancing clubs for banksters were the best, as far as I could see, that the once mighty British empire could offer me.

That night I took a Filipina girl back to my hotel, and my quest truly got under way. I had sex with her and took photos and video of her dancing. The next night I met her by chance in another bar with her friend and I fucked both of them together, the first time I'd had two girls at the same time in the same bed. Back home my sex life was almost zero and every pretty girl looked right through me as if I didn't exist, yet here in Hong Kong I was Shiva the sex god and only limited by the size of my bank account. Was I supposed to feel guilty and ashamed, as femprudes would want me to be? Well, sorry – I felt on top of the world and fully alive for the first time in my life!

Spike was right; prostitution was different here because it felt like natural dating. You just approached a girl in a nightclub and after buying her a drink and agreeing on a price, you took her back to your hotel and she'd usually stay the night with you. Often the girl would give you sex again in the morning. I had no illusions that the girls, with a few exceptions, actually fancied me of course, but that didn't bother me because I didn't want to get involved. I had to fight hard to see them as sexual objects. This statement, which appears to be sexist at first sight, is really the complete opposite of sexism: it is proof that prostitution is not shallow and mutually demeaning as so many contend. Sexual objectification is simply a natural first response to a member of the opposite sex after the first sighting. It is perfectly natural. It is what you do afterwards that determines whether its morally good or bad. Choosing an anonymous girl in a bar starts with 'sexual objectification', if you like, but as soon as you buy her a drink and start talking to her, it changes, because she becomes much more of a person, a fellow human being. The fact that a customer often has to struggle to keep this evolutionary process from gathering momentum is proof itself that sex with prostitutes is rarely about the cold, empty fuck. For many older men especially, it is a fight to stop falling in love with a sexy nymphet and getting caught in a very expensive honey trap and locked in to a draining relationship with Western Union! The Asian girls are often so sweet-natured and friendly that if I let myself see them as anything else but sex objects, I become infatuated with them. Despite this cautionary awareness, over the years I got involved with many of them and had many wonderful, albeit costly, adventures.

But now in my new-found Elysium I could really get down to business cataloguing Shakti's anatomical diversity. The goddess had an infinite number of avatars and they were all anatomically different. It was that difference that fascinated me, and I wanted to photograph it and express it in my art. I became a 'vulvic typologist', passionately looking to study the millions of permutations in the spectrum of feminine pulchritude. Every body type was deliciously different. Every breast, every face, every vulva, every anus was like a snowflake or a fingerprint in its idiosyncratic uniqueness - and I had to see that uniqueness. Every body I desired was a book I craved to read and add to my library. It was paradise on Earth for me. I had freed myself from the puritanical shackles of Victorian England – the land that for me was the land of sexual deprivation – and I had found my new home and destiny.

Nowadays youngsters get access to either relationships or uncomplicated sex on the social media through Facebook, Tinder and Instagram, but in my day I had no such easy access to women. I lamented my late start, but better late than never. I had a lot of lost ground to make up and although I wasn't exactly panicking, I was impatient. I felt so empowered I didn't just want to fuck women, I wanted revenge and justice; I wanted to stuff the whole bullshit world with a big spiked dildo right up its anti-erotic, baloney arse! Anarchy and contempt for body-phobic theology, which I felt had deprived me of Tantric fulfilment, now burned stronger than ever in my soul. I was in love with Shakti and at war with the world.

Why do I feel justified in holding such extreme ideas? Why is it right to deride Jesus Christ and Muhammad? I am justified because I hate pain, and monotheism is synonymous with torture and suffering while Tantra is about pleasure. The yab-yum and Tantric sex symbolise the pleasure principle and the concept of redesigning this world in order to make it a paradise for hedonists instead of a war zone of violence, poverty, injustice and suffering where few can realize their human potential. After a lifetime of studying these helllfire superstitions, I am convinced these men are theologically synonymous with torture. I'm not talking about the 'real' Jesus, whoever he was, I'm talking about the character described in the Bible and Church doctrine; this is the only Jesus who matters, because it is belief in this constructed Jesus that made Western civilization, to some extent, as calamitous as it is today. This book states the simple truth, but the truth is not actionable and almost unthinkable because to think it and believe it would necessitate rewriting Western history. It would call for the disestablishment of the Church of England, the abolition of faith schools, millions of Christians and Muslims being deeply offended - and this would only be the first step in the mass disposal of outdated mental habits. These conceptual deformities clutter up the Western mind and clog up the wheels of human progress. Public opinion, unfortunately, is not ready for such a radical paradigm shift.

It is the transgressive spirit of Tantra that appeals to me and suffuses my art. Tantra is a good example of thinking outside the box, and a counterbalance to political correctness. What is significant here, especially for my artwork, is that the sexual dynamic of male and female is deemed to be the very essence of the cosmos. Yes, I'm obsessed with women's bodies, but why shouldn't I be? They are the summit of visual experience. How can the monstrous regiment of bimbo feminists who want to abolish prostitution, erotic nightclubs and the male gaze ever empathise with the blood rush, the divine zap that a man can get from looking at naked women? Where are they coming from? Do they possess the moral high ground?

I'm all for women's equality, but if I'm going to be judged by others they have to pass a litmus test. I judge all my fellow human beings, especially women, by one golden criterion: do they know Jesus Christ and Muhammad threaten to torture trillions of people – half of them innocent women - for all eternity in the afterlife? Do they know this is plainly visible in black and white if they open their Bibles and their Korans? Do they know I want to paint pictures of beautiful women, not burn them in hell? Why pick on me, and men like me, for appreciating beauty? Can these patriarchal misogynists lauded as superheroes (who escape women's scorn for some reason) ever be theologically separated from their teachings of mass torture in the afterlife?

I know enough about the subject to know that the answer to my question is no. This is my priority. I want my women to be spiritually enlightened, and the first rung of the ladder to enlightenment is being a 'knower', namely someone who 'knows' that hellfire religion is wrecking the planet and we have to get rid of the sadomythic man in the sky. Christians will tell you they've already got rid of him and they now envisage God differently, but they still identify with Christ and the Bible, so the gesture is empty play acting. I am convinced the world suffers from a fatal 'hell blindness' and is living in denial of the fact that monotheism is a trinity of blasphemies. I make no apologies for my rational extremism or my justified obsession with hell. I am proud of being a rational fundamentalist because nothing else will divert this world from its collision course with doomsday except militant rationalism and a new Age of Reason. I've never met any woman or even heard of any woman who shares my condign aversion to the hellfire prophets, and it doesn't impress me if women are intelligent academics – in fact the more intelligent a woman is, the more she disappoints me with her inexcusable spiritual myopia. Since most of my darlings in Asia are either Buddhists or Christians I can hardly be blamed for being more interested in their bodies than their minds – or for being facetious at times!

The mythology of Tantric sex treats sexual love as a path to spiritual and paranormal self-empowerment. The goddess Shakti is configured as "kundalini", a snake coiled up like a spring of explosive sexual energy at the base of the spine. When the kundalini power is released through ritual sex and meditation and its power channelled upwards into the mind, it is said to bring the practitioner enlightenment and a range of supernormal powers. I have an open mind, but I personally don't believe this claim to be literally true. Nevertheless, it is a powerful metaphor to explain the way sexual love can energise a person to feel totally empowered and regenerated. Sex in Tantra then is a *way of power*. Sex as a metaphysical way of power is a difficult and unfamiliar concept for most people to accommodate, but this is what makes Tantra such a radical alternative to the platitudes of the church. The power of sex fills me with enthusiasm for life and inspires me to write books and paint pictures and to ask the deepest questions about the meaning of beauty and truth. It's important to grasp this point fully. Sex is not just a function of personal love, romance and marriage, important as these are to humanity; it is vital spiritual fuel, or pabulum. It is a solo quest for self- empowerment and a means of becoming psychosomatically energised. In a civilised society it needs to be democratised and made universally available to both men and women through legal prostitution - that is through voluntary, non-trafficked prostitution.

There is also a rational basis to the theoretical proposition that God is sex. This theory attempts to explain that if we take the scientific view of the cosmos as a vast organism running itself without the help of a Supreme Being, then it is justifiable to regard sex as a proxy creator, because in a sense it "creates" the universe by making it self-aware. Sex produces human beings who then "witness" the universe cognitively - otherwise the cosmos would not know it existed. Human beings endow the universe with "mind" or self-awareness, and it therefore is reasonable to say that God is sex. In this Tantric way of looking at sex it is seen as something cosmic; something much bigger than a mere expression of interpersonal love. Those who want to ban prostitution need, in my view, to factor these Tantric beliefs into the equation.

The feminist narratives that revolve around prostitution ironically underestimate the damage that patriarchy has done to both men and women. I believe prostitution in many parts of Asia, such as Pattaya and Angeles City, works as a relatively successful model or prototype for the future to improve upon. It's not ideal, but it provides a striking contrast to the entirely negative and jaundiced narrative promoted by the abolitionists. If you ask the average sex worker in Asia if she likes her work she is likely to answer in the negative. This is used wrongly by critics of prostitution as further evidence to support their case. We need to be aware of the fact that young Christian or Buddhist girls have been acculturated to be ashamed of fornication and prostitution. Most of them have lost their virginity, and as non-virgins or 'fallen' women they have had to suffer a denigration of their self-esteem from their own culture. For this reason they would not like to admit they enjoy their work, because they would be reluctant to admit they enjoyed sex with multiple partners outside marriage, let alone paid sex with strangers. Any woman, even today, who admits to casual sex is likely to be condemned by the double standard, even if she's not a prostitute.

Furthermore, what is sometimes overlooked by the feminist critique is an analysis of male sexuality and the male gaze that has taken into account how religion has damaged Western men. I believe that half the time men don't fully understand their own sexuality, and why they are often driven by their libidos. Most of the feminist reports, surveys and questionnaires processing men's anonymous sexual confessions are flawed, because they don't reflect the cosmic dimension of sex that is central to Tantra and might well operate at a subconscious level in the minds of many men. Those who are not attuned to the metaphysical side of sex may not be aware of the deeper and more meaningful reasons they are drawn to sex with prostitutes. I'm not saying the 'empty fuck' doesn't exist among shallow men with outmoded sexist attitudes but even superficial souls, who see sex in this way are to some extent victims of their culture, and the feminist narrative does nothing to address this issue and help men learn to respect themselves and the sex workers through spiritual insights.

The abolitionists define the relationship between client and sex worker as mutually demeaning. This is heinously pessimistic and is imposed on reality with the sinister intention of shaping reality to fit its own pseudo-intellectual distortions. I say to abolitionists - "I don't recognise your narrative because it doesn't square with my experiences." I ask them why the joy and laughter is missing from it; why there is no fun and dance? Personally I find the sex bars in Asia the most joyous and felicitous places on Earth, and that is because the girls themselves help create this atmosphere. When you go into the best bars in Pattaya or Angeles City you are hit with an exciting multi-sensory experience the like of which you might not find anywhere else in the world. There is a festive party atmosphere. All the bars are full of thumping beat music and creative lighting, coupled with themed interiors and personalised décor. Some of the bars are big and others tiny and intimate, and the girls are usually clowning around, dancing and giggling. When customers throw money at the stage they laugh and scream hysterically in the scramble to get their hands on it. It's an arresting sound, and even though it is only a faint vestigial intimation it reminds me of what I feel is the superior capacity women have for Dionysian ecstasy.

In pagan times women were much more in touch with this penchant for self-abandonment. Once I went out on my hotel balcony overlooking Pattaya Bay in Thailand, where I could feel, see and hear the palpable energy of the sex jungle. There before my eyes was the spectacle of hundreds of closely-packed bars, all full of girls and pumping out beat music, and above this glorious din the sound could be heard of naked nymphs and maenads screaming, caterwauling and laughing away the night until dawn. If these girls weren't enjoying themselves, they deserved Oscars for their acting. Do you ever find serving girls showing such effervescence in McDonald's?

I make extravagant claims for my art in this book, claims which some may view as overblown for someone who is not a famous artist. But that is perhaps the real issue. Is my work unknown to you because it hasn't been brought to the notice of Saatchi, or is it because it is not good enough to be celebrated in the glossy highbrow books written by erudite critics of the ethereal art world? Or is it unknown to you because the sexo-religious values of our society are so unenlightened and yet so entrenched in the public mind that people just can't see my work for what it is? I was trained at different art colleges, including St Martin's School of Art in London. Often I asked my fellow students or my tutors the million dollar question "How can you tell the difference between good and bad art? I never got a good answer, and now in my late sixties I have a stock of five hundred paintings or more that I have yet to sell. I saw in my newspaper only recently that Lucian Freud – an artist whose work I totally despise - has recently sold a painting of a grossly fat woman for £35 million! This for a celebration of ugliness in muddy colours and in dated style. He is lionized by some elements of the art establishment alongside Rembrandt and Rubens as one of the greatest painters of the human form.

As I write these words, London is hosting an exhibition of the work of Alexander Calder, who is credited with inventing the mobile. He apparently liberated sculpture from being static and grounded. All very well and mainstream. Anodyne art! How does that compare with the contribution my own work is making – a contribution nobody wants, because it means discarding treasured mental habits? My paintings are about the global replacement of infantile sex-phobic superstition with adult spirituality, which I think is more important than pretty mobiles. Sour grapes? No, I just want justice. In a world of universal deceit, to speak the truth is a revolutionary act. My art is a revolutionary act that goes unnoticed – a panacea that is lost like a piss in the wind because the world is blind. It's classic catch 22. I paint pictures to tell the world it is blind, but it can't see them because it's blind. The question I, and so many other unknown aspiring artists living in relative poverty ask, is this: if there are no objective values of good and bad art, why him or her and not me?

I regard the work of many 'successful' artists as derivative and inferior to my own, which is more original and conceptually profound. But who or what decides whether an artist is a "great" artist or not? Maybe with most artists living today it is about being connected, and the old adage is still true - "It's not what you know but who you know".

I am a qualified art teacher and I've been painting all my life and I know my work deserves critical acclaim. If this sounds defensive, it is only because I've had forty years of experience trying to get erotic art taken seriously and I've been unfairly censored in so many different ways and from so many different sections of society. Let me give you one example. I was flabbergasted when Authorhouse, the American publishers of my first book *Sex and the Devil's Wager* refused to use my cover proposal because it fell foul of their extreme puritanical policies. The image I proposed was unacceptable because it showed a nipple! I then had the same problem with my second book, namely *I Took the Sex Gods to Thailand*. At first Authorhouse assured me the cover design was acceptable, but later they completely reneged on this agreement. I had chosen to use the image of the yab-yum, a historic Buddhist and Hindu religious icon which is widely available to viewers old and young, in temples, museums, textbooks and on the internet. This idol, which was the inspiration for the title of the book and pivotal to the whole narrative, showed Shiva and Shakti in coital embrace. They are facing each other in a seated position and no genitals were showing, but the content evaluators objected to the slight intimation of what they laughably called Shakti's 'bum crack'! They also had a policy of not publishing images of simulated sex and this, in their eyes, disqualified my religious statuette! The yab-yum to many Tantrikas does not even signify sex in the literal sense but is a metaphor for cosmic non-dualism. This example of absurd body phobia, which has its many global counterparts in other cultures and locations, is in my view as good a vindication of the need for books like

God is Sex Not Sadism as any. They even refused to allow this image anywhere inside the book and compounded their stupidity by prohibiting a photo of a classic sculpture of Aphrodite that showed her breasts while allowing other photos of different statues that did! Not only was this a classic example of risible sexual censorship, it was also a marketing disaster. I could never come up with a better cover than the one they banned, which perfectly identified the subject matter of the book. Their nonsensical prudery, I am sure, reduced my sales and completely failed to provide the reader with an essential image of the sex gods to which the title of the book referred. I mention this example from umpteen that I could cite from my personal experience. They show the institutionalised body phobia that underpins the global delusion that we have sexual freedom, and the absurd assumption by so many religious leaders, politicians and anti-porn feminist campaigners that our society is too sexualised and awash with gratuitous sexual imagery.

Some erotic art does get the respect it deserves, but only if centuries of history act as a buffer zone between the past and our own times of internet pornography. The passage of time endows erotic art with a patina of social acceptability and dilutes its seditious message. Take Japanese Shunga art, which shows exquisitely-crafted explicit images of exaggerated erections, gaping vaginas and sexual intercourse, leaving nothing to the imagination. An exhibition of this art in London received rave reviews from intellectuals and art critics but these same commentators would not dare, I'm sure, express the same respect or interest in explicit modern erotica. There is so much humbug in the art world, which is now more than ever a money-driven machine serving parasitical art critics and private collectors. It is in my view largely devoted to gimmicks, oversized pretentious installations, shallow sensationalism and hype to feed the media.

Part of my motivation for writing this book is to change public attitudes and to make erotic art more mainstream, because it makes sense for it to be so. Considering sex is one of the most important human interests and concerns and is vital to the continuance of the human species, it is seriously under-represented as an artistic narrative and a cultural norm. Why can't erotic furniture, culinary products and erotic wallpapers etcetera, become as acceptable as their mainstream counterparts? In ancient Greco-Roman societies explicit erotic imagery was ubiquitous and normalised.

I unapologetically blame society for the fact that my work and the work of other underground erotic artists is not given the public and media attention it deserves. At one time I dedicated over a decade of my life exclusively to networking the media and presenting my work to umpteen art galleries, and all to no avail. I eventually stopped banging my head against this wall because I realised that it was a fool's errand to try and convince the establishment that my work was serious erotica and not pornography.

In short, even in the high-tech twenty-first-century, after thousands of years of cultural evolution, there still exists a global perception that images of an explicit sexual nature and especially the human genitals are obscene and socially corrosive and dangerous to children. I believe our

Judeo-Christian Islamic traditions are mainly to blame for the absurd body phobia that still blights our times. Judaism, Christianity and Islam have been throughout history, avowed enemies of paganism, and have seized every opportunity to behave as religious vandals destroying pagan idols and temples wherever they found them. The largely snobbish art world, which arrogantly likes to think of itself as anti-establishment, provocative, edgy and daring, rarely if ever has the courage to mock anti-erotic religion or push the boundaries of the uncensored body. Fearless erotica is still considered lowbrow art, and unfit for human consumption.

When the Iranian president visited the Pope in the Vatican in January 2016, the revered nude sculptures were covered up so as not to cause offence, and of course they avoided talking about the fact that Islam regards the Catholic doctrine of the Holy Trinity as the most offensive of all blasphemies! The sight of these two charlatans invested with massive power and influence, shaking hands drenched in the blood of history, was truly sickening to me. President Rouhani made a speech on this visit in which he repeated the mantra that is characteristic of Islamic propaganda in which he stated free speech should not be used as an excuse to offend religious sensibilities. In other words, he doesn't believe in free speech! This cynical sophistry is based on the false premise that the default definition of religion is entirely favourable and irreproachable. Religion has a very dark side, and just because believers can't see it doesn't exempt them from criticism and even contempt from those who can. It is also nauseating when Christians and Muslims whinge and whine about hate speech against their faith while completely oblivious to the fact that to pagans, unbelievers or ' infidels' the Bible and Koran are themselves the most extreme form of hate speech, defining them as hell fodder and in need of abject self-abasement and repentance.

I recall a massive annual erotica exhibition at Olympia where I exhibited my work a couple of times, along with several other erotica artists, but this event was highly commercialised and ideologically shallow, and to my knowledge never resulted in even one major art critic taking any of the art seriously. The exhibition was situated within a vast exhibition of porn merchandise from dildos to hardcore videos, and that's exactly where Big Brother wants erotic art to stay – as a genre of porn, where its revolutionary power can be neutralised. Even the nude itself as a traditional artistic motif is now avoided by most contemporary artists as being retrogressive and artistically exhausted.

In desperation, about this time, I tried to form a radical art movement that would have a religio-political agenda and a manifesto in the same way that, for example, the Italian Futurists of the early twentieth century painted works that expressed a revolutionary ideology. But I found no appetite for this among my fellow erotica artists, who lacked the vision or fire in their bellies necessary to take on the establishment and its antediluvian sexphobia. They were content to stay in their ghetto and make short-term financial gains. Despite the fact that I had many exhibitions and my work was featured on numerous television programmes and published in continental erotic art magazines such as *Nu* and sex magazines such as *Hustler* and *Forum*, I always found that these media agents, especially TV channels, had their own agenda. They usually tried to fit my work into boxes and easily digestible simplifications that kept it lowbrow and disarmed.

I believe, that as an erotic artist, I suffer serious oppression and censorship from the historical and cultural effects of monotheism. If it was just a matter of being anti-erotic it would not be so bad, but these death cults are much more dark and sinister than this because of their hellfire and damnation eschatology which literally sanctifies infinite torture. My point is this: if anti-eroticism comes from a good creditable source it needs to be taken seriously, but if it comes supposedly from divine revelations that define God as a monster who tortures his creatures mercilessly, can its body-phobic edicts have any credibility for the rational mind? The anti-erotic and anti-nudism stance of monotheism is based in grim sado-mythic superstition and yet still defines to a large extent the parameters of sexual freedom in the world today. I want to challenge this baleful legacy from monotheism, which to me is a spiritually retarded *zeitgeist* that is well past its sell-by date.

Even Buddhism's considerable anti-eroticism is rooted in hellfire. When in Thailand recently, I visited one of the "hell gardens", situated significantly in temple grounds and maintained lovingly by monks. It was crammed full of kitsch sculptures of 'sinners' and so-called sex-offenders subjected to every torture imaginable. These gruesome and lurid effigies are designed to terrify visitors and their children into good sexual conduct. Is it not time to ask questions outside the box? Does not the real pornography of our times reside in the blasphemy embraced by some religions, that God created a hell or cosmic Auschwitz? I'm a hedonist and I hate pain. We all hate pain, so why are we all so unconcerned about religions that claim it is God's right to inflict unimaginable pain on us for all eternity? Hinduism and Buddhism may well have their hellfire teachings which should be questioned, but they are not so theistic. In Eastern religion, hell is more akin to a dark side of nature processing the effects of karma as a natural law. But in monotheism you get the iniquitous dynamic of a Supreme Being who is supposed to be loving, merciful and just, yet who consciously tortures his own creatures for no good reason and with no end in sight and no hint of rehabilitation. Strangely enough, this quite obvious abomination, which is closer to kindergarten mathematics than rocket science, escaped the attention of the giant intellects that composed the Universal Declaration of Human Rights, which seemingly ignores the human rights of the resurrected!

I'm sure most people don't see the point of religion bashing. It seems a futile endeavour, because no one can prove God doesn't exist and religion is obviously here to stay, because whether it's true or not billions of people seem to need it. The problem is that all debate and dialogue has dried up. In times like ours when no one challenges religious belief, believers become arrogant and too sure of themselves. If believers are never made to doubt and question themselves by critics outside their comfort zone, they become prone to fanaticism, and fanaticism can breed terrorism. Islamist terrorism is fuelled by a fanatical faith that has never been properly exposed to the brunt of militant rationalism.

My art is not about denying God but about replacing the sadistic gods of wrath and vengeance common to monotheism with a rational model of God. Obviously this can't be done overnight. But I can make a fresh contribution to a new debate altogether, one the world desperately needs in an age when religion has become so political and dangerous. Feminist spirituality is arguably defunct, and atheism has nothing to contribute to the debate any more; it is now, like feminism, shooting blanks. It stupidly picks a fight with God instead of religion itself and its false models of God.

Added to this, interfaith debate is also pointless, because the different theological positions are all equally right or equally wrong and cannot produce a correct or definitive verdict. They are based on faith and not facts or evidence; any interfaith debate is therefore a closed circuit and a waste of time. The question whether the Bible supports the doctrine of the Holy Trinity or not, for example, can never be answered conclusively one way or another.

But what about rational believers in God – the somethingists? What about a belief in God that is not based on faith but on reason, and simply defines God as the Absolute or the Ineffable or the numinous mystery at the heart of the universe – the generic Core Reality? Maybe people who reply to the question "Do you believe in God" with the answer, "Well, I believe in *something*" are the true believers of the future. I define myself as a somethingist, which is pretty much a position based in mysticism. Maybe God is a Supreme Being or maybe God is the universe - who knows? The jury is still out on this matter.

I'm open to any concept of God, whether it be deist or theist, in fact anything plausible, but not the God of hellfire. This is not a position of vagueness, but of humility and tolerance. Such an all-purpose God, one who does not have to be a Supreme Being but is conceptually open-ended, can provide a real and unprecedented challenge to conventional religion and hopefully start some constructive debate again that political correctness has hitherto almost managed to stifle completely.

Let me just explain why this idea of Tantric rational religion is so revolutionary and such a threat to monotheism. Progressive Christian liberals will tell you they themselves have evolved similar rational concepts of God but they still self-identify as Christians, which means they have not cut themselves free of the Bible and hellfire. They want their cake and they want to eat it.

Atheism fails miserably to debunk religion because it tries to prove the impossible, namely that God does not exist. But it further disempowers itself by narrowly defining God according to the 'enemy's' definition of God as an anthropomorphic Supreme Being. This is evidence of both ignorance and irrationality, because much of Eastern metaphysics defines 'God' with the impersonal pronoun 'It' or pantheistically as the universe, or simply as Ultimate Truth. But added to this, I have a crucial advantage over the atheist in kyboshing monotheism: I have the silver bullet. To the atheist there is arguably no such thing as blasphemy, so he cannot accuse monotheists of being blasphemers. But to me, a believer in a rationalistic God, blasphemy is very real. I can then in the debate with Christians and Muslims accuse their hellfire

God of being blasphemous – an accusation I can back up with ironclad logic.

In my Tantric worldview, the view expressed in my art, God breathes through every image and brush stroke, but there is no hint of hell and damnation. There is only love of God and life; only love of truth, dance and sexual ecstasy. I would like to state as a preamble to the pages that follow, some of which are devoted to consolidating my case against false religion, that in my last book, *I Took the Sex Gods to Thailand*, my best friend Spike is a Catholic. Virtually all the girls I bar-fined whether in Thailand or Philippines were either Buddhists or Christians, so my critique of religion is not hate speech but tough love, and my whole impulse and motivation is merely to stimulate debate and to break the gagging order that seems to want to protect religious sensibilities at the expense of truth. I believe in the maxims 'hate the message not the messenger' and 'hate the belief not the believer', and I am proud of the fact that I despise Christianity and Islam unreservedly, because it is the duty of civilized people to hate anti-God hellfire superstitions that block mankind's progress, or worse. If most Christians and Muslims are good people, as they are, this is all the more reason to help them out of their darkness by showing them the benefits of Tantric paganism. I hope my paintings will help to show them the errors of their ways. In fact I see my paintings as more than paintings; they are didactic religious icons that reveal the face of God. I am a pagan preacher.

I want to save God from superstition and relocate the concept where it belongs within the magisterium of science, art and philosophy. What I am trying to do is identify the principle 'enemies' of erotic art and sexual freedom and hopefully debunk their wrong-minded narratives. These threats I believe are certain religions and certain elements of feminism. I am now, as a man who pays for sex, defined in the laws of some European countries as a criminal. This deeply offends me and annoys me because it is outrageously unfair, not just because it is morally wrong but because many of those who define me as a criminal are vectors of grossly immoral ideas themselves. This is why I devote considerable space to exposing religious evil.

But what, you may ask, has hell got to do with feminism? My answer to this is that feminism promised us a new vision of God that could improve on the sadistic Patriarch in the sky, and it failed miserably. Not only this, but individual feminists who wish to abolish prostitution and slander men like me for wanting to look at strippers and go-go dancers are often themselves Christians or secularists who have unconsciously been influenced by religious bigotry. The significance of this is that feminism has completely lost the plot, and lost all sense of proportion, causing it to get its priorities fatally wrong. My thesis, which I attempt to justify in chapter two, is this: why has so much of the feminist critique been directed at sexual objectification, pornography and prostitution while largely ignoring the misogynistic sadism of religion? Why have so many feminists attacked the attitudes and behaviour of men like me and not the quintessential example of male violence and cruelty which is instantiated in hellfire religion? Men like me love good-looking women for their erotic beauty, but Jesus and Muhammed want to burn them in hell, and still feminists choose to attack us instead! Why are they silent about hell and soft on patriarchal religions that define millions of women as potential hell-fodder and 'sinners' or infidels deserving infinite punishment? If patriarchy is about gratuitous male violence, which is often directed at women, and if it is about cruelty and violation of human rights, then what greater example of this is there but the teaching that the "He" God is a mass torturer?

I am not going to produce a thorough proof that the Bible and the Koran teach this abomination because it is beyond the scope of this book. I have actually already published a book on hellfire theology, but I can assure the readers that after a lifetime of research I am left in no doubt that the holy books teach a literal belief in hell and eternal torture and there are millions of Christians and Muslims living now who agree with me. If I am right, and I'm sure I am, I can then argue quite rationally from this premise that feminism must take some of the blame for the rise of Daesh and Islamic terrorism!

Impossible, absurd, you say? But surely feminism promised us a new vision of God, and it hasn't delivered. Over the last forty years or so it should have vigorously attacked the credibility of the sadogods of monotheism, and it failed miserably. If it had managed to successfully challenge the patriarchal shibboleth of unconditional religious freedom which requires no rational quality controls, if it had debunked monotheism through proving religious sadism targeted women in the afterlife, it might have destroyed the pro-religious matrix that allowed the revival of Islam to take place. If even some Western countries had embraced a new ethos that was hostile to hellfire superstition, the foreign policies of America and Europe might have been very different. Perhaps we would have been far less likely to oppose more secular Muslim rulers like Saddam Hussein, Gaddafi and Assad if the alternative is highly likely to be Islamic theocracy and sectarian violence.

Feminism allowed the beast to live and thrive unchallenged, and now it is free to continue its mission unhindered. Feminism failed to bring about the preliminary stage of the new Age of Reason, and it must therefore take some responsibility for the global propaganda scam that is now being conducted by most politicians, journalists and academics that Islam cannot be blamed for Islamic extremism. It is one of the worst conspiracies in the history of Western civilization that steadfastly proposes that there is a fault line or firewall between, for example, ISIL and British Islam. Muslim extremists all emphatically self-identify with Islam, and the desire for a caliphate is one of the central tenets of Islam. ISIL is arguably just another *valid* theological interpretation of Islam like any other. Radicalisation is not a mental aberration that doesn't belong in true Islam – it is just one more expression of Islam's natural political fundamentalism. Around 800 AD Muslims invaded India and by some estimates slaughtered 400 million Hindu pagans. During the occupation, which lasted for centuries, survivors were enslaved and castrated, raped, deported as slaves and forced to convert. The massacred were literally turned into hills of skulls. Muslims burned whole cities to the ground, and of particular interest to me, they destroyed hundreds, perhaps thousands of beautiful temples and priceless pagan idols. Yes, and David Cameron, who is Prime Minister as I write these words, assures us that Islam is a religion of peace and that ISIL are "monkeys, not Muslims". One is forced to wonder how many British MPs have actually read the Koran.

There is no supreme or overall authority in Islam to decide which interpretation of Islam is right and which is wrong. I could give a hundred examples of how ISIL and moderate Muslims might be equally justified in their interpretation of Islamic scripture, but I will give just one example to illustrate my point. Moderate British Muslims, apart from continually claiming that Islam is a religion of love and peace when history and scripture tell us otherwise, say Islam teaches that suicide is *haram*, or forbidden. This is true, but Abu 'hook' Hamza, the British hate preacher who advocated the killing of unbelievers, argued that suicide bombings are not suicide in the normal sense of the word. Most suicides are arguably cowardly acts where God's gift of life is thrown back in his face and therefore insult God, but a suicide bomber serves God by sacrificing his life for a holy war or jihad. Suicide can be suicide or it can be 'martyring', which is very different. Both these interpretations are perfectly justified in the Muslim world view.

Islam has spawned a host of savage monsters to rampage across the world and ISIL is just one of them. Others will follow until the cancer of political correctness is cut out and Islam itself is held accountable. In chapter two, I will cite support for my thesis that feminism has failed women from Mary Daly, who is arguably the most seminal mind of the whole feminist movement.

There is, I would be the first to admit, a dark side to pornography and prostitution, but this book is about highlighting the good side. I want to emphasise the positive side of the sex trade to establish a counterbalance to the official establishment narrative, which is already well known and in my view largely delusional. I believe the dark side of the sex trade is not intrinsic but largely the result of the failure of the authorities to stamp out trafficking and abuse. Prostitution is bedevilled by incidental defects caused by old fashioned sexism, criminal exploitation, and the tendentious narrative of the censors themselves.

Mainstream feminism has treated sex workers most often with condescension and disrespect. But voluntary sex workers are arguably true feminists, defying the sexual prohibitions of patriarchy. Reactionary feminists and do-gooders actually exacerbate the problems they are purporting, in their self-righteous ignorance, to solve. The orthodox narrative actually stunts the growth of the sex trade by never allowing it to evolve, mature and re-invent itself in the image of a new vision of human sexuality. It was the feminist revolution that was supposed to provide this new vision of human sexuality, yet it has completely failed to do and has come full circle. With only a slight change of rhetoric it has ended up climbing into bed with the religious puritans who also condemn nudity, prostitution, pornography and the male gaze. This religious condemnation of the male gaze, known as "adultery of the heart" in Christianity and "fornication of the eyes" in Islam, has been given a new name by feminism and regrettably a new durability, namely "sexual objectification".

I try to ask questions through art about the relationship between erotica and pornography and where red lines have to be drawn. I am also passionately involved with the whole issue of prostitution, because the zeitgeist of the modern era seems to be hardening in its attitude to prostitution and not only using people trafficking as a justification for pursuing abolitionist policies, but now actually criminalising the act of paying for sex. The general trend in Europe today is arguably moving in the direction of criminalising men like me who pay for sex as sex offenders and felons. In the minds of increasing numbers of liberal bigots and misguided moralists, I and others like me are deemed as criminals and accused falsely of exploiting women and reducing them to sex objects stripped of their humanity when we pay for sex. I find this really vexing, and it has prompted me to research the history of prostitution and the arguments for and against. I believe I can make a unique contribution to this otherwise stale and circular debate by using a Tantric perspective.

The Asian sex market, especially in Thailand and Philippines, is ideally suited to the Tantric sex pilgrim who wishes to practise his worship of the feminine form and its rich morphological diversity. It confers unlimited bounty on the sexual adventurer who has no moral reservations about using non-trafficked sex workers and seeks access to inexhaustible numbers of beautiful young dancers who often operate in Asia, contrary to public perception, in a relatively safe, congenial and convivial environment.

In the Philippines, where there is a high level of Catholic prejudice against condoms, leading to all sorts of problems, most of the hassle and harassment of the bar owners and the girls comes not from customers but from police raids and police corruption. Obviously the police have to check the bars for drugs and underage girls, but it is well known that they have an ulterior motive, which is to collect bribes.

All the problems I encounter with UK escorts are caused by the asinine laws that define my relationship with them. It is because the escort business functions in the face of hostile establishment values without any outside regulation or accountability that girls may be mistreated and customers are often deceived. The girls in the galleries are sometimes completely transformed in Photoshop to such a degree that it can only be described as immoral deception. When they turn up they are sometimes far older and less attractive, or even completely different individuals who bear little or no resemblance to their gallery pictures. Choosing an escort on the internet in the UK is always a hit and miss affair, and for me it has resulted in many very negative experiences and expensive mistakes. Feminists may complain that an Asian bar is a cattle market where girls are put on show but the girls are not selling themselves. They are selling a sexual service, and it is only fair to the customer that he can see what he's buying.

Even when you see the girl in front of you, you never know what you are getting until you get her back to the hotel. Club lighting, or lack of it, and costume design can hide a multitude of sins. I am unashamedly looking for a premium body to inspire my art and only fifty per cent of the girls I have chosen ever met my rigorous criteria. Personally, as far as corruption in the escort business is concerned, I believe that cosmetic enhancement is already enough of a deception and to protect customers further, the unfair digital erasure of all imperfections needs to be addressed.

In Asia I have had personal relationships over the years with many of these girls. All of them had chosen this work because it paid better than other options, and all of them insisted to me that they were not trafficked and their work was voluntary. Many are looking for a foreigner to marry and provide for them and most are free to leave their chosen vocation whenever they like, and I know girls who have done so. I'm not saying there are no exceptions to this general rule or that there are no dangers to sex work, but these are exaggerated by detractors. My art is thus a plea for the decriminalisation or legalisation of this noble profession, at the very least, and a call for nothing less than a sexual revolution through which Tantric insights are embraced and incorporated into the social fabric of our times.

Apart from London escorts booked on the internet, my art is almost entirely sourced in Asian prostitution where bar girls and go-go dancers provide the stimulation for my unique genre of erotica. A defence of the principle of paying for sex and the right of adults to freely engage in this activity as a transaction of mutual benefit forms an important part of this book.

Some people have a romantic idea about erotica. They think it has something to do with subtlety and artiness and 'good taste', but erotica in my definition means something far more vigorous and robust. It references the whole all-inclusive world of human sexuality but with a moral conscience and compass that seeks a direction towards truth and better understanding between men and women.

My art clearly defines the difference between erotica and pornography. Erotic art can be multi-dimensional and deeply conceptual, meaning it stimulates the mind as much as the body. Pornography on the other hand is at best a somewhat banal aphrodisiac or a visual aid to masturbation, and at worst misogynistic drivel. Feminists are right to point out that most of pornography depicts the subordination of women, but they are reluctant to talk up its many good points, one of which is the way internet porn showcases the feminine body. Its presentation may be tacky most of the time and even degrading to women on occasions, but it is the first time in the history of the world that the man in the street has been able to access a visual lexicon of body types from the infinite spectrum of feminine pulchritude. I see all these women as diverse manifestations of the feminine principle which is instantiated in the goddess Aphrodite. On my laptop at any time of day or night I can enjoy looking at strippers performing for me, usually free of charge, and showing me all the beautiful details of their unique anatomy. Enjoying this aesthetic elite, this tiny minority of women who turn me on, in no way degrades my general view of women as my social equals.

From a Tantric perspective, this internet access to feminine bodies is a very positive and awesomely beautiful side of pornography. It is belittled and scoffed at by anti-porn detractors, even when it is known that these strippers are not ill-treated or coerced into this line of work and like many prostitutes and other women in the sex trade, simply want to be accepted, respected by society and left alone to continue their good work. There are in fact at any one time millions of women who have freely chosen to work in the sex trade, whether it is prostitution, go-go dancing, porn movies or modelling, or simply working from home selling webcam sex. These women are perfectly normal and intelligent and are not victims or brainwashed sex slaves, but that doesn't stop society stigmatising them and misrepresenting them in the media.

We can fight rape, domestic violence and sexism; we can fight the subordination of women without depriving men of their God-given right to appreciate the beauty of nature - and what better example of natural beauty is there than the female body when it is young and well-formed? At risk of overplaying my hand, I reiterate that feminist activists should focus on the male sadomythic arrogance that claims to know the mind of God. Men who claim they know what God thinks and how he wants us to behave, then go on to give themselves a mandate to boss women around. These charlatans are the real archvillains of male supremacism, but most feminists are not even looking in the right direction. Instead, feminist spirituality today has lost its way and is no longer about finding a new direction, but grovelling to male oppressors in the churches and the mosques to get reformist scraps and concessions and positions of power in the patriarchal Armageddon machine.

My artwork is a challenge to women, especially Christian and Muslim women. It asks " How can you be so naïve as to believe men who claim to know what God thinks?" and "Why do you worship a male, bossy, God who thinks your sisters in their trillions deserve to be resurrected to torture because they don't share your beliefs when there is no proof for your beliefs? Why don't you convert to paganism that is sex-positive and simply based on love of life and the universe?" Paganism respects women as adults who are free to define God independently of misogynistic clerical interference designed to preserve male privilege.

I earn my living as a musician and songwriter, and the same message of spiritual renewal is written into my lyrics. So my paintings should be viewed as part of a package that has different elements which, when combined, present a coherent and plausible prescription for change. I don't of course expect to actualise any great changes in my lifetime, merely to plant seeds that will germinate truth-seeking in others. I argue that my erotic images carry a Tantric message that is nothing short of revolutionary and transformative. Each art form has its limitations and paintings alone cannot accomplish great change, but I promote my message not just through my art but through my music and my books. My paintings may look indecent to some, but actually they are highly conceptual – in fact unapologetically didactic. I call this genre 'conceptual erotica'. It forms an accompaniment to my book writing and song writing. My paintings cannot be construed apart from my worldview, hence the publication of this book and others.

Conceptual art, as the name suggests, is a genre that attaches great importance to the ideas or concepts that underpin the image itself. In fact the concepts are often held to be the whole essence of the work. Any image is possibly semiotically infinite, because everything in the universe is interrelated, but to understand images in artwork, the viewer must be familiar with the artist's ideology and intentions. My works have a visual content that contains many contentious images, and most images in art are interwoven inseparably with many social and metaphysical issues. Someone viewing my work for the first time will see both photographic and painted images of the female anatomy, juxtaposed with images of Tantric gods and goddesses and various visual references to Tantric ideas and pagan idols. My works are profoundly prescriptive, and punctuated with slogans and aphorisms that load the images with political and spiritual significations offering solutions to the world's problems and guidelines for the spiritual renewal of humankind through Tantric Humanism.

No doubt upon seeing my work for the first time viewers will make their own judgements, but I want to make sure that if these judgements are coloured by misconceptions and prejudice, I can at least help them make a more informed assessment. What any erotica artist fears is a knee-jerk reaction from the viewer who might well have been socially conditioned to see all vulvic imagery as automatically pornographic without studying the context or the intended meanings. It is for this reason that this book offers discourse on many subjects that I feel directly relate to my work. For example, anyone who wants to look beneath the surface of my 'canvas' (I actually use hardboard) will realise I am unashamedly obsessed with the beauty of the feminine form, and have been pleasurably addicted to it all my life. But how does my beautiful monomania relate to the feminist critique of the male gaze and sexual objectification?

The sexual objectification of women is a natural human reaction to the beauty of the feminine form. It is quite likely that the average red-blooded heterosexual will, upon seeing a beautiful woman, feel sexually aroused and curious about what she looks like naked, and this instant natural reaction happens before he knows anything about her. Surely when this takes place it is a case of sexual objectification? What is wrong with this, and what is wrong with taking it further and watching striptease on the internet or in a lap dancing bar? The male gaze is morally neutral until it takes a path right or left. It can lead to respect or disrespect to women depending on who is doing the gazing.

My immediate defence would be to argue that feminism has identified a problem that we are attempting to solve by thinking in the wrong place – a gender-specific cul-de-sac that pressures men to be ashamed of celebrating women's beauty and sexuality. It arguably makes more sense to encourage a gender balance where women are persuaded through sensible argument to celebrate male beauty rather than to demonise the male gaze. This has actually been proposed by some feminist writers, because it could very well be that men discourage women from sexually objectifying them because they fear being judged, especially by the size of their penis. Maybe men at a subconscious level like their bodies to be powerful and even dangerous to women to keep them in their place and deter them from laughing at them. Perhaps men have discouraged or even trained women through the ages not to sexually objectify them, as this would encourage them to behave more like men and be more promiscuous, arousing jealousy and casting doubt on their children's paternity.

The fact that rape is still practised by men despite greater public awareness of this social evil makes it difficult for women to have a completely positive and loving relationship with the male body. This is why I believe we need a much more probing debate about rape and its causes, because Tantric principles cannot work effectively until women can feel comfortable loving and respecting the phallus or lingam in the same way men love the yoni. A summary glance at internet porn reveals a male obsession with genital anatomy that I believe is well justified, but to close the gender gap this beautiful erotic addiction needs to be reciprocated by women.

The double standard that condemns women for wanting to have equal sexual freedom with men has been famously sustained and rigorously enforced down the centuries as a blatant ideology of female repression. No wonder the male gaze is so gender-specific. I am in a constant state of sexo-spiritual tension as I see beautiful women all around me; women who give me rapture by their beauty but angst because I cannot make love to them! Held in thrall to this dynamic I know I am alive! I want women to feel this emotional intensity – to share in my "aliveness".

Maybe it is time for a more public emergence of the female gaze to revolutionise human sexuality! I think the feminist movement has failed to appreciate the positive side of the male gaze, largely because women in general do not arguably share men's love affair with physical beauty; they do not feel the same passion for male nudity that their male counterparts feel for the feminine form. I think this is one of the main challenges I face in trying to explain my work to women who cannot easily relate to my public display of their bodies. I want women in the future, especially older women, to better enjoy the benefits of Tantric sex with young male sex workers. I look at it like this - even if the male and female brain are hard-wired differently, they can do the same things in different ways. If women nowadays are taking up male contact sports, even cage fighting or full-contact mixed martial arts, then is there any reason why they can't explore the female gaze and demand equal rights with men in this sensitive area of human sexuality?

What I would call 'anti-erotic feminism' arguably makes the mistake of assuming that the worshipful love of feminine beauty on the one hand and the respect and recognition of women's equality on the other have to be mutually exclusive. Why can't men be allowed to adore the feminine form as an epiphany while at the same time respecting all women for their intellectual and moral equality with them? In Tantra, the sexual objectification of women is considered to be a good and wholesome thing that celebrates feminine pulchritude through reverence and respect for God's supreme masterpiece, namely the human body and specifically the feminine form. There is also a whole tradition in Tantric Hinduism and Buddhism of yoginis or female adepts and shamans enlightening men through sex and their physical beauty. In a similar way sex workers energize and enlighten me by providing the spark plug that galvanises my creative and intellectual endeavours. The concept of erotic dancers and prostitutes enlightening men through their skills and services is not something feminists have taken seriously enough.

Tantra sees the whole universe in terms of yin and yang and human sexuality in terms of the male and female principles. These principles are defined, not so much by secondary markers relating to the psyche, but the primary markers of the physical. Male and female are defined predominantly by their physical differences - the most emphatic being the genitalia. It is for this reason that for centuries religious art in Hindu temples has depicted the vulva and the phallus as divine symbols. It is therefore logical from the perspective of this world view for men (and arguably women) to be initially more interested in appearance than inner content, which is far less gender-specific. When a man sexually objectifies a woman he sees her beauty as a light that momentarily dazzles him; her inner self is still all there and of vital significance, and he knows it and doesn't have to be reminded all the time by his feminist critics. All journeys begin with the first step, and for many men the first step is to enjoy the primal feminine principle expressed as 'body' or appearance. Later on, love may demand an engagement with all aspects of a woman's being, but it all begins with the male gaze, which is perfectly natural and to be defended against sex-phobic religions and feminists devoid of Tantric wisdom.

My art is rooted firmly and unashamedly in the male gaze – the gaze Jesus Christ condemned and equated with adultery of the heart as in Matthew 5:27. Jesus arguably taught that the male gaze, fornication and adultery are deadly sins deserving eternal physical torture in hell. This is hate speech against men like me, and Islam doggedly follows the same script! I am proud to call myself a dedicated Antichrist and defender of God and sexual liberty. ISIL are absolutely right when they say the multi-faith society doesn't work and so now we have to choose between the caliphate and the age of Aquarius. ISIL's caliphate may perish, but the caliphate itself is an idea that will threaten us for as long as we tolerate Islam. Islam and sharia law are intrinsically dangerous and will always pose, in my view, an existential threat to our freedoms.

Given the wonderful complexity of human psychology, is it not possible for men in a post-feminist age to see beautiful women to some degree as sexual objects (or as I prefer 'sexual idols') while at the same time recognising their less gender-specific qualities? I think it is possible for men to have this dualistic thinking, and the love of a minority of women for their beauty is not incompatible with an equal love of their collective humanity. Surely it is time to evolve out of this ridiculous war zone where sexualised images of women have to be banned and women covered up in order, as many Muslims and feminists contend, to protect their modesty and intellectual status!

Defining a tiny minority of women by their external appearance or beauty need not automatically cancel or diminish their inner personhood, and nor should it be interpreted as a slur or commentary on women in general. It's worth repeating that I don't believe the so-called sexual objectification of a tiny minority of women a man might be attracted to has a massive impact on his attitudes to women in general. Women as a whole are never sexually objectified; there is no necessary transference of sexual objectification from a man enjoying a beauty contest, for example, to the general population of women whom he regards simply as fellow citizens.

I can explain my position better on a personal level. When I see a beautiful woman I don't assume she is dumb because she is beautiful, or forget for one moment that men and women are equal, and nor does she represent all women or any generalised characterisation of women by men. I think it is only natural that this tiny aesthetic elite, which for me includes women of many diverse shapes and sizes, and which is personal to each man, is given credit for possessing a seductive surface charisma that momentarily mesmerises a man in its transcendental light. The instant and most immediate markers of the feminine principle are in my view anatomical and about physical appearance. Men and women 'look' very different, so why shouldn't this play a vital role in the process of men recognising women as women?

In Tantra a desirable woman under the male gaze is not objectified but idolised or literally idolatrised, because she is 'elevated' into an avatar of the goddess Shakti or Aphrodite. Iconolatry is the worship of icons, and to me a beautiful woman is a divine icon – the imago dei. Women may protest they don't want to be put on a plinth and worshipped as goddesses but simply to be respected in the home and workplace as equals, but what harm does a man do by extending his respect to include a little sexo-spiritual adoration?

My work is best defined as feminine iconolatry. It is not reductionist; it doesn't deny the woman's intellect or personhood – it merely regards these qualities as less tangible and largely inexpressible in the visual arts. I can't paint a woman's intelligence, but I can faithfully reproduce a clear image of her anatomical assets. Sight is instantaneous. Beauty impacts the senses in a fraction of a second. The inner person or the psychological profile, is relatively speaking gender-neutral, because it is less representative of the primal energies of the male and female principles. I feel it is worth repeating that these are represented in Tantra by the male and female sexual organs or the lingam and the yoni, and that in Hindu temples the vulva and the phallus are ubiquitously represented as elemental cosmic forces and are depicted by erotic sculptures. In prehistoric times when the Mother Goddess was almost universally worshipped, the vulva was a religious icon or ideogram etched into rocks and caves as a symbol of birthing power and cosmic creation, but in our sad, deluded times public depictions of the vagina are considered reductionist, indecent and demeaning to women.

It is often the anti-erotic feminists who are the most sexist. They condescendingly ignore the protests of sex workers and strippers who simply want their work de-stigmatised. Instead of respecting these women, many of whom are well educated or even political activists, they generally dismiss them as bimbos who have masochistically internalised patriarchal value judgements. In fact it is anti-erotic femprudes who suffer from Stockholm Syndrome.

My book is important, because not only does it explain why paying for sex is a vital service that society should condone and even encourage, it exposes the hypocrisy of the global art market, which has an appalling track record when it comes to representing erotica. My book calls for a revolution in the art market by demanding that art galleries have the courage to show more art that deals honestly, and if need be, explicitly, with sexual issues. Erotica is at the same time the Cinderella of the art world and its enfant terrible. Fundamentally, the art world is a microcosm of global culture which reflects humanity's infantile fear of the vagina and the erection, as if images in the public domain of these natural God-given body parts automatically become pornographic, dangerous to minors, and a threat to public law and order. Tantra asks the world, "Why are we still not free to enjoy the uncensored body?" Why do TV stations warn their viewers about nude content in the movies they broadcast when the nude scenes are so redacted they don't even show the genitals or realistic copulation? Why is there an 'adults only' warning signalling danger on every kind of public showing of erotic images? Islamophobia, implying there is no such thing as a rational fear of Islam, is a dangerous myth, but sex-phobia is a morbid threat to rationalism and common sense.

I'm not suggesting the world should become a giant nudist camp, only that society should make a genuine effort to offer a more positive and less paranoid narrative about public nudity. Why, for example, can't all beaches be open to people who want to be natural and naked? I think I can make a very constructive contribution here to what I perceive as a serious global social problem that is ignored by most of us. Many people lament the fact that children learn bad things about sex from internet porn. Surely this is because we offer them no alternative? When do we ever send a message to youth that there is nothing wrong or shameful about nudity? Part of the remedy for this shortfall in our pedagogic duty could be to incorporate tasteful but explicit erotic imagery into sex education from infancy.

I know how reluctant the money-driven art world is to take erotica seriously. Many of the big art collectors now are from Arab Muslim countries where explicit erotica would be totally unacceptable. Most Muslim, Christian, Hindu and Buddhist countries, and even non-religious countries like North Korea and China, share a paranoid fear of edgy erotic material. In a post-feminist age, even so-called secular countries are little different in their attitudes to sex and nudity from their religious counterparts. Erotica is considered a dodgy and risky investment for art galleries eager not to offend religious or feminist sensibilities.

Yoni puja is a Tantric term which quite literally means vagina worship, based on the idea that women's bodies are incarnations of the goddess. In Tantra the posture of a naked woman with splayed thighs is a sacred image of female power and is called *uttanapada* because it is both the position for sex and childbirth. In our society in most contexts it is considered sexist and smutty. My art is certainly a form of yoni-puja which as I hope to demonstrate is quite natural in Tantra but considered almost a form of sexual perversion in my own Christo-Islamic culture.

I am not insisting that the only source of sex phobia is religion, because secularists have negative attitudes too, but I do believe religion is the major contributor to our sexual hang-ups. In a post-feminist age that has alerted us to the institutionalised ubiquity of patriarchy, it is important not to throw the baby out with the bath water. Tantra is unfortunately patriarchal, like every religion, but let this not blind us to its fresh insights, and I'm especially thinking of yoni puja. In a sense the pornsphere on the internet is a crude form of yoni puja where we are entertained by countless women willingly showing their private parts. My art work is forcefully thematized by love of the vulva and the anal starburst as natural forms that are fascinating to me, not just because of their sexual significance but for their beauty and morphological diversity. In Tantra the yoni is the abode of the goddess – the Shakti locus and the twin mouth of cosmic creation and procreation. Both the yoni and the lingam or penis are revered for their procreative power.

My schematised images of the anal rosette or starburst are based on extreme close-up photographs of this highly erotic part of the female anatomy. Such magnified images show the anal starburst as a fascinating complex natural form, and each lady has her unique anal morphology that offers the artist infinite diversity. But my calculus would be that no art gallery would accept the anal motif as anything else but a smutty joke. For me it is a clear case of the failure of the art market to sometimes live up to its mandate to push the boundaries and promote cutting edge art even if it might offend. The anus, like a fingerprint or snowflake, has infinite permutations, and it goes without saying that it is a vital functional part of the human body and I, like many men I'm sure, find the feminine buttocks very erotic and can enjoy anal sex when offered. It's also a very politically-charged part of the human anatomy and at the heart, surely, of the gay revolution. Anal sex has been a capital offence in many countries at different times in the past and is still illegal in many countries.

So to conclude, the anus is a natural form, performing a vital biological function, and can be beautiful to an artist, and last but not least, it is sexually and politically charged. It should surely be accepted as a fit motif for the artist. And should it not be taken seriously by art critics and public alike? I am sure from anecdotal evidence that most men have at least thought about asking their wives, girlfriends or their call girls for anal sex at some time in their lives. Many men secretly desire to experiment with anal sex, but it is still a taboo subject outside of the pornsphere. The female anus is figured prominently and ubiquitously on internet porn, which proves one thing at least, that there is a huge appetite among men who watch porn for this beautiful erogenous zone. If we assume that porn watchers are not all sex perverts but that most of them are normal people from all walks of life as they are, this demonstrates a large public interest in this part of the female anatomy. But this widespread internet fascination with what I would define as 'anal aesthetics' is ignored in mainstream culture and never talked about or reflected in art. I believe my ground-breaking work makes me the first serious artist to use the anus as a valid motif.

At the time of writing this book, the UK has been racked by multiple sex scandals involving high-ranking politicians and retired celebrities who have abused their position of power and influence to force their sexual advances often on minors – the most notorious being Jimmy Savile and Gary Glitter. These terrible examples of child abuse have also now come to light in the wake of what is arguably institutionalised sexual abuse in the Catholic church and historic paedophile networks in Parliament and children's homes. In such unfortunate circumstances there is now understandably little or no sympathy for older men such as myself, seen as sex tourists, seeking sex with young women abroad. What possible rationale could there be to justify such behaviour? This is why it is more important than ever for the public to hear a completely different narrative. I argue that in an ideal world where Tantric insights are respected and considered actionable it would be deemed a good thing for the elderly of both sexes to keep sexually active. Once it is accepted that Tantric sex as a unisex methodology is uniquely beneficial to human health and welfare, it is logical to demand a society that provides access to sex workers who can provide the necessary service, for which they would be well paid and deeply respected by all concerned.

My quest for Tantric sex with young foreign women is based on the need for good health and longevity, the love of beauty, and despite the cynical disbelief of sceptics, ultimately the quest for truth and enlightenment. Many of the young women I meet tell me they prefer older men as customers because they are more respectful and appreciative. My relationships with these girls are based on abject gratitude, respect and real affection, and I hope when I have expanded on this issue in future chapters I can present a persuasive case for prostitution which will establish greater all-round understanding.

I also think that public perception of prostitution would be far less characterised as a form of male sexual deviance if women, especially older women, were also regular customers using male dancers or escorts. The phenomenon of women who pay for sex has historical precedents and is actually increasingly practised in our own times. If prostitution was decriminalised and made socially acceptable I am sure many more women would be encouraged to use male escorts. My artwork and the philosophy it expounds is highly supportive of these advances in sexual equality. I like to think my paintings are important ideograms whose function is nothing less than a revolutionary proposal or panacea for radical spiritual renewal through Tantra-based ideology.

Despite the emphasis I place on physical appearance for my work it should be said that every man who seeks to have a good experience with a sex worker knows how important it is to find a girl with a warm heart; the intelligence for good conversation, and above all a good personality. Without these considerations, enjoyment of her body will be blighted. This is why in the bars of Asian red light districts the customer is always advised to select a girl first on appearance but then to buy her a drink in order to talk to her and sound her out to ensure she has an inner beauty to match her outer comeliness. If I was looking for love and a serious relationship then all the internal aspects of my selected mate would be of vital importance. However in my Tantric quest I am not looking for love but to use primal, elemental feminine beauty and its infinite permutations as an energising and inspirational force in my quest to understand life. I regard the go-go dancers I meet and make love to almost as semi-divine beings, like the *apsaras* of Hindu mythology: they are my umbilical cord with the feminine principle, my fallen angels from heaven, without whom I could not properly practise my religion or create my art.

I regard myself politically as a transitional anarchist. By this I mean that before a world government can be established, a period of no-nonsense anarchistic deconstruction would have to take place. For me, Western civilization is spiritually and ideologically bankrupt and therefore moribund. This world is a doomsday machine - a delusional reality system that has been largely manufactured by three of the most villainous and hurtful men who ever lived, namely Moses, Jesus and Muhammad. One of the slogans I use in my artwork refers to these men as 'superbugs', which I'm sure most people would find quite shocking, but that's how I honestly see them – superbugs that continue to defy all known antibiotics. I don't know why Greco-Roman paganism failed, allowing the Christian takeover to eventuate, but I wish fate had chosen something better than Christianity as a successor. Christianity may have started out being less cruel while it was an underdog but it soon changed when it got power and hegemony. The superstitions these men have propagated are pessimistic death cults prophesying the premature, supernatural end of the world. They are arguably self-fulfilling prophesies that have brought the world to its present crisis, and it is this madhouse that I escape from through sex with young, beautiful women. My girls are symbols of peace and love in a disgusting macho, war-riven cesspool of human corruption and stupidity – dystopian reality. When I take a sweet nymphet back to my hotel and penetrate her silky tunnel she not only envelops my penis in bliss but my whole being in spiritual rapture and freedom from Realpolitik. I can momentarily forget that I'm living in a psychotic bear pit owned and run by spiritually-retarded politicians - my intellectual and moral inferiors. For a few blessed moments the evil world is cancelled out and I float in the empyrean. But of course, to my would-be detractors all this is humbug and fancy rhetoric to disguise the simple 'truth' that a man like me who demeans himself by going with a prostitute is just trying to dignify the proverbial 'empty fuck' with depth.

The famous sculptures of Aphrodite were inspired by a beautiful prostitute in ancient Greece whom the sculptor believed had the body of a goddess. I view the vast majority of women as ordinary human beings – pleasant interesting people, as are most men, but mere mortals none the less. How does it demean women in any way if I take spiritual inspiration from a minority of their sisters who to me look like goddesses?

I would also like to make it clear that the worship of feminine beauty is not about one exclusive beauty ideal. The models I depict in my work come in all shapes and sizes, and anatomical diversity is a cause for celebration. The beauty ideal may not be all-embracing and totally inclusive, but it allows for a broad, colourful subjectivity and multiple permutations.

CHAPTER ONE

Dancing Whores

Tantra offers the beautiful metaphysical poetry of Shiva –
a mighty God covered in cobras, dancing with Shakti in
shamanistic rapture and at times making love. Shiva
dances the universe into existence, and in time he will
dance it into destruction and oblivion. Dance and sex are
defined as the essence of the cosmos. In Tantra the essence
of the cosmos is joy and desire, not sin, judgement and
damnation, as it is in the death cults of monotheism.
Tantra not only proposes the primacy of sex but divinizes
dance, elevating it to a sacred cosmic activity. Shiva in his
dancer aspect is called Nataraja. Whenever I see women
dancing, this association of primal sex and cosmic dance
suffuses my mind and I am unapologetic in admitting that

I am totally intoxicated and addicted to the greatest show on Earth, namely the naked feminine body moving to music.

My paintings all celebrate dance and dancers as an essential part of the Tantric quest. Each work is a separate personal tribute to a dancer I chose after viewing her dancing on the stage. This is the essential magic of Asian prostitution, which is rooted in ancient temple dance. On my last few visits to Angeles City in the Philippines I have been impressed with the effort many of the bars are putting into choreographed dance routines for the girls, and dance groups are now an integral part of the sex scene. In Angeles I witnessed some amazing athletic pole dancing. Some Thai and Philippine bars can boast anything up to two or three hundred naked or semi-naked dancing girls who are also available for sexual service.

Most people do not associate prostitution with serious dance, but historically speaking the two are intimately linked. The fact remains that for me they represent the sacred Tantric link traceable to Shiva and Shakti creating the universe from their lovemaking and ecstatic dance. I see my girls in a timeless parade of feminine pulchritude, forming a continuum; a chain of profound kinetic symbolism originating from prehistoric, shamanistic Shakti dancing, through to the heavenly apsaras.

These Asian apsaras are supernatural shapeshifters who can assume any number of permutations in the feminine spectrum and are thus able to satisfy any male fantasy. They are both erotic dancers and seducers of mortals, but they have their human counterparts who wish to emulate them, and temples in Cambodia were at times well populated with real-life apsaras who have been immortalised in temple bas reliefs. The modern day apsaras in Cambodia provide entertainment for tourists but offer no sexual service like their forbears. This is left to go-go dancers in the bars of Asia, who I believe also carry on the legacy of the apsaras in their own way, even if their dance style is somewhat different!

In Thailand I have often witnessed girls running naked in the bars and banging on the tables, performing a Buddhist ceremony to bring good luck and prosperity. From their point of view there was no intention to be sexually provocative. They do this whether customers are there or not. But of course seeing these naked nymphs all running like Dionysian maenads is just as much a turn-on as the dancing on stage. In Thailand the religious connection still exists in many of the sex bars, although one can't imagine that Buddha would be very happy with the association. When I look at a go-go dancer in Thailand or the Philippines I see this pagan heritage and I see the goddess in each girl dancing for peace and love in the world. In stark contrast to this illustrious pagan legacy, dance plays no meaningful role in the theology or mythology of Christianity:

If dance is legitimate at all, and particularly if it is legitimate in worship, we must admit that the New Testament evidence is nil and the Old Testament evidence is sparse....If the Word of God does not specifically condemn dance in worship, it certainly does not command or encourage it either. (*Shall we Dance*, P.66-67, Brian Edwards)

My paintings are a chronicle of my personal Tantric odyssey through Asian bars and brothels, and they not only fuel my creativity in the arts but energise and direct my quest for understanding God and my destiny. I could easily save a great deal of money staying in London, where I could find professional models for photography shoots without travelling abroad for sex workers. Alternatively, I could save even more money by using the masses of free pornography on the internet, but this would not be enough for me. In the sex bars of Asia you get a real experience of Tantra which describes sex as a way of power. You really feel the high voltage energy of sexual love when you enter one of these bars. At their best they pulsate with the life force. For me they are heaven on Earth.

In Tantra the analogy of the body as a temple is taken seriously. When I dedicate a painting to the beauty of a woman, I want my art to be personal; I want to have made love to her. I need to enter the temple in order to consummate my act of worship. My need to 'possess', to unashamedly 'claim', the woman I eulogise, and the fact that as an OAP I cannot find young women by dating, makes paying for sex the very cornerstone of my sex life, my art and my religion. The word 'possess' is no doubt problematic for some feminists, especially the late Andrea Dworkin, and I will explain what I mean by this more fully in chapter four. My work therefore by its very nature is a vehement protest against the centuries of unjustifiable persecution and vilification levelled against sex workers, and now I hasten to add, directed at me and people like me for paying for sex. Adults should have the right to make their own arrangements and informed choices about the conditions that pertain to their sexual acts.

Sex workers are like fallen angels. They are to me

beautiful rebels defying the laws and prohibitions of their puritanical masters – the sacerdotal patriarchs in the churches and mosques. With their wages of sin they feed themselves and their families and as sex donors they share their inspirational beauty with strangers who need it. They are the lost children of the mother goddess who once in prehistory reigned supreme and was represented by the ideogram of a vulva etched into the rocks of Mother Earth, and these votive icons still survive to this day to tell of better times before Abraham, Moses, Jesus and Muhammad brought the sado-religions to terrorize the earth with threats of a lurid resurrection from the grave and torture and damnation for outsiders. Like the fallen angels of the Bible who were seduced by the Promethean spirit of Satan and the snake, I see them as demi-apostates occupying a no-man's land where they are held hostage as sinners. These fallen angels, are I believe, the modern manifestations of a powerful dynasty of erotic angels in the evolution of the world. We can only imagine what women's pagan dancing was like in the time of the Mother Goddess.

Although men have in a sense hijacked female dance for their own concupiscent purpose, it is fair to say that beneath the male expropriation of female dance, the core essence can still be sensed, if not seen, where dance is women's esoteric expression of spiritual independence. If this lost knowledge could be retrieved, women, I believe, could seriously change the world through using dance as a form of political protest. I believe women should use dance as a protest against state authorities, especially Muslim countries like Iran, that restrict their right to dance wherever and whenever they like. Dance is the ultimate expression of joy and the love of life.

The young Thai and Filipina girls I choose from the dance stage to make love to can sometimes be persuaded to dance in the hotel room. Sometimes they even let me video them, and from these videos I can take stills for my paintings. They are often innocents from the provinces and have no idea of the noble profession they have unwittingly taken up. As erotic dancers, they are automatically transmogrified in my eyes into iconic apsaras or ancient temple dancers. Their erstwhile sisters from temples in distant centuries and distant lands were once arguably shamanistic sex donors, but now all positive and sacred connection with the temple has been lost and replaced only with monotheistic shame and guilt. If they have low self-esteem resulting from their work, it is largely because society tells them it is demeaning work instead of praising them for their sexual hospitality.

Indian temples are renowned of course for their erotic sculpture, where hundreds of voluptuous semi-naked dancers are on view, in, for example, Konorak and Khajuraho. In Buddhist and Hindu mythology, *yakshis* are seductive forest nymphs and *apsaras* are beautiful heavenly dancers who can can fly. The fact that apsaras are shapeshifters is a concept that has deep philosophical implications for my art and my sexual worldview. My addiction to feminine pulchritude can only be explained by reference to apsaras, because it is as if all the sex workers I possess are in fact the same woman who has changed her shape and personality to show me some of her infinite permutations.

The apsaras may not have the royal status of Aphrodite, but they too represent the feminine principle or the goddess and invoke the metaphysical fantasy of a beautiful woman adopting numerous guises while in the act of making love to you. The temple apsaras were at times the most numerous and exotic dancers in Asia, especially in the famous temple of Angkor Wat in Cambodia. I personally visited this temple and was amazed to see nearly two thousand individually-sculpted dancers in bas relief who represented the harem of the kings who had a royal palace within the temple grounds. In my paintings I often juxtapose images I brought back with me from Angkor Wat with images of their divine sisters - my dancing go-go girls. Angkor Wat was one of my most profound sexo-spiritual experiences. These bas reliefs are heavily stylised and are great works of art which manage to crystallise the essence of feminine dance. To be in the company of nearly two thousand semi-naked stone beauties and to imagine their real life counterparts in the heyday of the temple, moving around the grounds, was a mind-blowing experience.

Temple dancers were not always just valued for their appearance and sexual gifts. There is a serious tradition in Asian religion that recognises women as shamans, or transmitters of divine enlightenment. This is why my paintings are full of images of these semi-divine beauties who in my mind are represented by my beloved bar girls and go-go dancers. Although the go-go dancers cannot enlighten me through any shamanistic transmission, they enlighten me with their beauty and yin sex-energy that fills me with awe and wanderlust for knowledge about the universe that has evolved such pulchritude. To me they are the peacemakers and the living apotheosis of that wonderful slogan from the sixties: *make love not war.*

In Tantric India, beauty had a transcendent quality. A man or woman was brought near to the divine by the degree of his or her beauty, and only inevitable human imperfections prevented such a person from actually being divine. Only a statue or god or goddess is a perfect embodiment of transcendence. The idea of heaven came totally to dominate Indian art and religion as a sexual paradise full of apsaras or celestial sex sirens for dead heroes. On earth, the hero warrior kings had harems of beautiful girls, many of whom would have been spoils of war, and heaven was just this earthly model perfected and projected into the sky. Sexual completeness was considered the primary precondition for spiritual completeness, which could best be achieved if sex was indulged in with multiple partners.

Apsara dancing in Cambodia dates back more than a thousand years. During the great Khmer empire, dancers performed in temples. The apsaras in Angkor Wat were concubines of the king and the origins of the apsaras in Hindu mythology are closely associated with the snake and the quest for the elixir of life. Their role was so revered that the king created the Royal Ballet to act as intermediaries between the monarch and the spiritual realm. They lived within the palace and represented the soul of Khmer culture. Dance was deemed a celebration of the gods who themselves are cosmic dancers, and every dance was considered an offering to them. In an art form whose origins are said to be divine, the performers are a link between the earthly and the heavenly realm. Dance evolved with the construction of Hindu temples, the greatest being my beloved Angkor Wat in the twelfth century. Dance was integral to these beliefs, which is why it was so generously represented on the temple walls in the form of carved apsaras. The temple was a recreation of the Hindu cosmos, and the dancers symbolised its rhythms. They were auspicious channels between the gods and the king who had to rule justly and provide for his people.

Shiva's cosmic dance, ushering the world into existence at the beginning of a creative cycle and destroying it at the end, reinforces the fundamental principle of dance as divine activity. The Hindu perception of time is cyclical, not linear and creation is thus a continuous process. With the image of a god as dancer, dance itself is an offering to the gods and a continuation of cosmic rhythms. ...Dance and drama have been fundamental to societies throughout history. They reflect not only the myths of a culture, but religious and political views, highlighting events that relate to the worldview of the audience, rendering them even more poignant. (Denise Heywood – *Cambodian Dance.*)

In the 20th century this dancing heritage was almost destroyed during the genocidal Pol Pot regime, when in Cambodia ninety percent of the dancers were murdered. The Taliban have also been known to murder women simply for dancing at celebrations in their villages. They are arguably the religious version of Khmer Rouge, hell-bent on taking the world back to the Stone Age or year zero. Only sadistic maniacs could kill dancers who bring peace and love to the world. Go-go dancers are to me peace messengers, like their predecessors – a living protest against male violence.

The tyrannical rule of the brutal Khmer Rouge under the dictator Pol Pot began in 1975 and caused the senseless murder of millions of innocent people under the insane policy of Year Zero. In the Maoist rural 'utopia' these degenerates hoped to create, there would be no more art, dance, music, songs, laughter, education, or telephones. Cambodia was turned into a vast forced labour camp. Only a few dancers survived to carry on the traditions. There were 300 palace dancers before the Pol Pot regime, but only thirty returned to rebuild the repertoire and many of the dances were lost forever.

Apsara dance is arguably the quintessence of femininity, which I see as a manifestation of human gentleness and love. This may be an idealised and old fashioned concept of what it is to be feminine but these dancers perfectly embody it and I believe it is important that it is preserved and treasured. In a modern world of male violence, where women are increasingly pro-active in the world's armed forces, I think it is important not to lose altogether this alternative feminine ideal of the delicate flower-like pacifist. In Cambodian dance, the face remains serene and smiling and dance becomes a haunting celebration of slowness. It seems to slow the process of time, like clouds drifting across a summer sky with hypnotic subtlety. Because the dances are so slow and the movements and gestures relatively small and measured, the eye has time to fully appreciate their elegant beauty.

Over a thousand years ago 64 temples, called *yogini* temples, were built in India, dedicated to Shakti the ultimate Tantric goddess. A yogini is a shaman or mystic and is portrayed generously in these 64 yogini temples as seductive large-breasted voluptuous women who impart enlightenment and wisdom to men often in a package of empowerment including sex. The yogini, also known as Sky-walker and Space dancer, is often a woman who bestows enlightenment on men through her sexual generosity. Some of them are sculpted skilfully as dancers. Wisdom *dakinis* can be human female gurus or goddesses of many kinds. For example the Diamond Dakini is a beautiful singer-cum-dancer with a voluptuous body, and coupling with her results in the 'Great Bliss' orgasm and brings prosperity and rebirth as a god. The iconographic representations of dakinis show them as young naked figures in dramatic dancing poses and sometimes with wrathful faces. It is said that only females can awaken the Muladhara chakra, the seat of kundalini serpent power.

One sacred mantra addresses each of the 64 yoginis in very sexualised terminology, and here are some of the Tantric appellations or titles that reveal the deep erotic connection between the goddess, shamanistic power, and sex. These temple yoginis are addressed as yogini with golden body; yogini ruler of physical pleasure; yogini lover of passion; yogini ruler of seminal essence; yogini essence of sexual fluid; yogini sensuous goddess; yogini giver of upward ecstasy; yogini desire itself; yogini snake goddess; yogini of shining rapture; yogini of dripping yoni; yogini residing in semen; yogini intoxicated goddess of heaven; yogini energy of the yoni; yogini of the sacred erection; yogini guide to bliss; and last but not least, yogini with beautiful yoni.

The goddess Ishtar, who was often identified as a prostitute, was the great goddess in the Middle East from 3000BC, and wherever she was worshipped sacred prostitution was an integral part of holy ritual. Babylon was a centre of temple prostitutes and many specialised as singers, musicians and dancers. Astarte was the Phoenician version of Ishtar. She was a goddess of love and fertility, depicted as a beautiful naked woman, and is associated with the infamous Jezebel who is slandered in the Bible as a pagan harlot when in fact she was a Phoenician princess who challenged the religious arrogance of the Israelite priest Elijah. Elijah, no doubt carrying out orders from Yahweh, finally managed to get her killed and eaten by dogs. Her assassination is seen as a metaphor for the triumph of Judaism over the 'harlotry' of pagan polytheism.

Ancient Greece had state-run brothels and at Corinth, Aphrodite's temple was staffed by over a thousand whores. Hetairai, arguably the most sophisticated of Greek whores, were often rich and educated, and were muses to great artists and mistresses of emperors and kings wielding political influence. In classical Athens, male-only banquets were a popular and frequent occurrence, and the men were entertained by groups of dancer-musician-prostitutes called the auletrides, or flute girls. These amazing women were sometimes gymnasts who played flutes, drums and finger cymbals and performed the sensuous dances dressed only in loin cloths. After the feast, men often enjoyed the sexual services of the dancers.

The most famous auletride was Lamia, who was mistress of kings invested with wealth and political influence. The Athenians even built a temple in her honour, deifying her under the name 'Aphrodite Lamia'. Another famous lady of the night was Phryne, whose lovers included many famous artists and who modelled for the celebrated statue of Aphrodite by Praxiteles. Aspasia was equally famous and intellectual, almost ruling Athens, it was said by some, through her lover Pericles. Sometimes auletrides and hetairai indulged in their own single sex gatherings, which were all-female banquets and festivals at which the participants both honoured their goddess, Aphrodite, and their calling with much lesbian activity.

In ancient Rome there was a rich medley of diverse sex vendors. Acca Larentia was a legendary Roman courtesan who left her sizeable fortune to the Roman people and was later deified and revered in a festival. Bustauriae were quite bizarre, as professional mourners who prostituted themselves in graveyards between funeral gigs and fornicated on tombstones or in crypts. This bizarre custom is better understood by referencing Tantric philosophy in which sex and death are bookends of reality and a sacred dynamic dualism. The binary of sex and death is a familiar concept in the West but in Tantra it is more than a concept – it is a deep visceral sentiment and way of feeling.

Dorides were in-call escorts who stood naked in their doorways - an erotic spectacle that I regret I will never witness, like so many lost gems, and which only the unlikely eventuality of time travel will ever bring back or retrieve from oblivion. Flora was a Roman goddess with a whore aspect and in her public festival, prostitutes would strip naked and perform erotic dance until male onlookers would join in making what can only be described as a public orgy. Lupae, or she-wolves, were wandering streetwalkers who attracted their clients by making wolf cries. We can only imagine how erotic, transgressive and beautifully pagan such creatures must have been howling for sex and money! Aphrodite, as the whores' protector, continued to be worshipped in her Roman guise as Venus. Her temples were often schools of instruction in sexual techniques similar to Indian Tantra.

In Tantric rituals in India the priests often intoned the mantra, "Looking upon a prostitute is a virtue that takes away sin"; prostitutes were considered auspicious and going with them could cleanse one of sin. The temple dancers were known as *devadasis*, the daughters or 'slaves of God' and often used *rathi mudras* or special erotic hand gestures symbolising different sexual acts. The dancers I have hired in the bars and I celebrate in my work are, as I say, the metaphysical relatives of the ancient temple dancers or devadasis of India, and the fabulous apsaras of Cambodia at the temple of Angkor Wat. The religious connection has been all but lost and all nexus with the goddess gone, but the fundamental spirituality of the greatest show on earth – the erotic dancer – can never be erased or lost.

The archetypal and iconic essence of this tradition is the femme-fatale dancer – the abiding signifier. Sacred prostitution is not highly valued by many feminists, because whereas it dignifies prostitution by linking it to divinity and endows dancers with 'mana' or spiritual power, it nevertheless takes place within a patriarchal context, so any dignity afforded the temple sex workers is still contaminated with masculinist value judgements. It is true that temple prostitution, which at the end of the day prioritises men's needs, is not an ideal, but it is nevertheless an index of how prostitution is not necessarily always a matter of street walkers giving blow jobs by the roadside to finance their drug habits.

Temple women were often used both as donors to the temple and as dancers in festivals, but not all temple women were dancers or prostitutes. The devadasis were considered numinous by many Hindus before Christian colonialism. One idea I love is the concept of the devadasis as *prasada* or vehicles of auspicious divine power. In Hindu worship after an offering has been made to a deity it is automatically sanctified, and if it is distributed amongst devotees it imparts prasada, allowing them to share in the divine presence. The idea that a temple woman is a form of prasada rests on the notion that a woman belonging to the deity might also be enjoyed sexually by the worshippers of that deity and that such a woman would thereby act as a kind of conduit of divine favour from the god to his male devotees. The idea of a temple woman being a donor is also of interest to me. I see go-go girls as givers: as blood donors giving me new lifeblood, or as sex donor-vendors, giving me yin power to merge with my yang and create the power surge, the alchemical zap of the life force. I get a psychosomatic power surge that I feel throughout my entire body when I choose a dancer, and know that in the wink of an eye I am going to see her fresh as a daisy emerging from the shower room of my hotel about to reveal all her mysteries at the drop of a white bath towel.

The dance girls gave to the mother goddess by supporting the living temple. They donated to their families and children by donating their bodies to men. They donated to the goddess by selling her to the world as evangelists and dance-preachers, selling her as the feminine principle of peace and love. By dancing and donating their bodies to men they earned religious merit. The temple prostitute is more a product of royal chieftains ruling as divine kings. The court and the temple became one, serving the needs of the god-king. In India, especially in Tanjore city, the kings had massive *seraglios* with many concubines. The dancers were used as entertainers in court functions but also in court rituals. Many of the dancers were deployed in temple rituals and others in the palace to entertain the colonial British. Some of the songs performed by the courtesans were highly erotic or salacious. Many temples supported dancing girls who underwent rituals of dedication to temple deities, but a large number of non-dedicated dancing courtesans did not participate in religious ceremonies but had non-conjugal sex and danced at the salons or weddings. Some of the dances were amazingly erotic, involving complex symbolism and songs of erotic lyricism, and the dancers would sometimes suddenly break out into song. Other dances were about comparing parts of the female body to aspects of nature. This Indian genre was arguably the most advanced, semiotic dance style that has ever existed.

The devadasi was an expert in dance, singing and the art of love. She was generally better educated than any other women in her society. With God and King as her chief patrons, she often became rich and powerful. Her community included dance teachers or gurus and musicians. Devadasis regarded it as a great honour and privilege to be slaves of god. Their dancing symbolised sensual love and mystic union with the divine. They were auspicious icons of the erotic and the spiritual. They were in the King's entourage and often performed at weddings and social functions. All over India statues of the courtesan dancer were evident.

Devadasi were often used in Tantric rituals, and some of the palaces employed up to 16,000 dancers. Victorious kings demanded dancers as booty after victory in war, and reinstated these talented women in their own palaces. Devadasis were often generous when rich, making donations to the temple and even building temples, wells and gardens. They commissioned master sculptors to make gold and bronze statues of gods and goddesses to be installed in temples. They were taught a multitude of skills beside song, dance and painting. These arts were called 'kalas' and even included making love-potions.

Kings saw no shame in using courtesans as auspicious conduits to the divine. A courtesan was a divine priestess connected to the meanings and mysteries of the universe through her dance and her sacred vagina. The oldest erotic dance in the world is belly dancing – originally a fertility dance practised in the temples by the ancient Egyptians and it is imitative of copulation. The act of sex was sacred and the fertility of the land linked to the fertility of the Pharaoh and his kingdom. The temple dance rituals were sacred and often ended in the act of copulation. The dancer would perform for the deity she was worshipping with her back to the audience; dancing released a sacred energy in her which enabled her to form a link with the deity, so she became a medium of the divine for the men in the audience.

Strippers in history, who are often dance trained, have struggled against public prejudice to get their art respected. They have often had to defend their craft as an art in the press and law courts. Luz del Fuego, a famous Brazilian stripper and feminist, founded the first Brazilian naturist camp and danced with snakes. Burlesque fuelled the development of the striptease through long-legged blonde showgirl dancing. The Folies Bergère in Paris in the 19th century had courtesans dancing on the stage, and sex workers paraded in a promenade behind the stalls. In Paris the prostitute was elevated to the status of performance artist and the brothel to the status of the theatre, and even the licensed brothels in Paris were offering sexual performances.

The cancan dance derived ultimately from ancient fertility dances. The French cancan was performed in the dance halls by a chorus line and in the Moulin Rouge the dancers exposed their crotches and underwear. Montmartre was an oasis of candid Bohemian humanism in a Victorian universe where women's hot sexuality was steaming through dance and fornication and nude modelling for famous artists. Louise Weber, said to be the founder of French cancan, was also a prostitute and a vulgar sexual revolutionary. She became a populist sex symbol when painted by Toulouse-Lautrec, who caricatured her gestures in the posters which launched Le Moulin Rouge. She represented the link between sexual consumption and erotic dance. She also chose her lifestyle to escape the drudgery of manual labour and working-class bondage.

Burlesque adopted a fusion of dance styles – the couch,

the shimmy (which involved rippling of the body from head to toe) the bump, the grind, and last but not least the Hawaiian hula dance. These were styles picked up at World Fairs. Salome became the symbol of the new woman – strong, assertive and destructive. Fine art nude painting influenced sexual attitudes by giving rise to the art of living statues or *tableaux vivants* where women imitated the poses of figures in well-known classical sculptures and paintings. The 'life model' was the erotic sensation of the nineteenth century and the precursor of the erotic dancing of the twentieth century, and the law required the model to remain motionless – here the criterion that divided art from porn was movement. But by the beginning of the twentieth century the moving picture industry was transforming eroticism by making recordings of sensual dances like belly dancing. It was said that most women in burlesque were professional prostitutes.

Burlesque was a uniquely American art form. The stripper puts her personality into the act, unlike a showgirl. The emergence of the showgirl was a new concept. They were exhibits situated in the continuation of a long tradition of Western art, of the painted nude and the performance of living pictures, they were put on display, whereas erotic dancers displayed themselves.

Soho, offering striptease in the UK, was riddled with crime, gangster's rip-offs and corrupt policemen. Before 1968 strippers were not supposed to move when fully naked, but gradually strippers got totally gynaecological, which led to seedy peep shows. Strippers could now be sex workers, photographic models and porn actors. The anti-pornography movements began in the 1970s, when WAVAW (women against violence against women) took direct action against sex shops, and sex workers of all kinds found themselves alienated from the feminist Anti-Porn Movement, which considered them victims. Feminist women allied themselves with the Anti-Porn Movement and declared it their intention to 'reclaim the night' to make it safer for women to walk the streets. The live action of the strippers was replaced with the passive body of the peep show artist, where men pushed coins through slots in a booth for a glimpse of pink. The militant sex worker - the strong confident salacious stripper, the 'bad girl' - was replaced with the very representation that feminists had campaigned against – the passive object of the male gaze. Negative images of women were reinforced: the victim, the fantasy object, the empty fuck. Through this sexist feminist fascism, women were denied their hard-earned right to horny behaviour, lust and longings to seduce.

CHAPTER TWO

The Feminist Antichrist

There is a bond, then, between the significance of the women's revolution as Antichrist and its import as Antichurch. Seen in the positive perspective in which I have presented it, as a spiritual uprising that can bring us beyond sexist myths, the Antichrist has a natural correlative in the coming of the Antichurch, which is a communal uprising against the social extensions of the male Incarnation myth, as this has been objectified in the structures of political power. (Mary Daly, *Beyond God the Father*, P. 140)

The above statement from the radical feminist Mary Daly

propounds the revolutionary idea that feminism could, and perhaps should, reconfigure itself as the Antichrist dedicated to the disarming and deconstruction of patriarchal religions. I believe the best way to negate Islamic extremism and the apparent credibility of its fearful anti-erotic sharia law is to douse the flames of Islamic triumphalism. Fanaticism thrives on unquestioning self-belief. This hubris, this unshakable conviction that the Koran is a perfect book of wisdom, incentivises terrorists. Islamic intolerance of dissent and criticism has resulted in many religious assassinations of writers, journalists, bloggers and artists who have 'offended the prophet'. This religious fanaticism will continue to expand until Islamic over-confidence is challenged with militant rationalism whereby critics are allowed to expose the many phobias and defects in Islam without incurring death threats.

Mary Daly, arguably the most radical and revolutionary of all the feminists, would certainly have disapproved of my attitudes to women, prostitution and sex, but when it comes to religion we are pretty much on the same page, united in our militant rationalism. However I would like to point out that even she seemed to miss the full significance of hellfire and damnation for women's issues. She coined the magnificently subversive phrase "If God is male then male is God." This succinctly describes the inimical process by which a self-proclaimed prophet on behalf of the male sex projects his alter-ego into the sky and re-names it God, which then gives him and his male followers the right to boss women around, or as Daly puts it so eloquently:

Males have tried to rid themselves of their impurities by subliming themselves into "God," who is "sublime," and who is so lofty that he really is nowhere and thus can be said to be everywhere. The earthly/unearthly males have vaporized and then condensed/reified their self-images into the sublime product, god, and they use this condensed and purified product as a mask to engender 'awe.'........ (Pure Lust, P.73)

And she repeats this insight in *Beyond God the Father*:

Patriarchal religion adds to the problem by intensifying the process through which women internalize the consciousness of the oppressor. The males' judgement having been metamorphosed into God's judgement... (P. 49)

The new wave of feminism desperately needs to be not only many-faceted but cosmic and ultimately religious in its vision. This means reaching outward and inward toward the God beyond and beneath the gods who have stolen our identity. (P. 29)

But if God is male and God is defined theologically as a mass torturer of women in the next world, then it follows logically that male power derived from this God is by definition personified violence, injustice and sadism. If the tyranny of male power defined by religion is essentially stealth sadism cloaked in lip service to love, we therefore need to eradicate it. When you introduce hellfire theology into the equation, when you introduce eschatology and the mass posthumous torture of women into her famous mantra, it becomes awesomely subversive: the algorithm that can finally destroy the beast of patriarchy.

From being a Catholic theologian, Daly eventually came to self-identify with paganism and denounced monotheism as irredeemably patriarchal. She went on to propound the radical thesis that women will never be liberated until they cease from trying to redeem and reform the male gods (the most notable being Yahweh, Jesus Christ and Allah) and have the courage to call for brave new God-models to serve the whole of humanity and not just men. She wants women to explode with "female fire" and "volcanic powers". She sees the final wave of feminism "hurling forth Life-lust, like lava, reviving the wasteland, the World." The feminist cause which is based on achieving equality with men is in fact, according to her, fool's gold, because equality with men is merely equality in the dubious privilege of helping to run the doomsday machine. By getting equal rights women gain short term improvements, but in the end, without the root and branch deconstruction of patriarchal, male-defined religion, history is doomed to endlessly repeat itself until the cycles of war and anarchy eventually bring about the end of the world. An apocalyptic doomsday is pretty much ordained as a self-fulfilling prophecy embraced and fuelled of course by monotheism.

But Daly's potent radicalism doesn't stop here. As we have seen, she even suggests that feminism itself is the true manifestation of the Antichrist! What a delicious thought: woman-spirit-rising like a tsunami, finally drowning the world's most psychotic nightmare – resurrection and damnation.

I suggest that the mechanism of reversal has been at the root of the idea that the "Antichrist" must be something "evil." What if this is not the case at all? What if the idea has arisen out of the male's unconscious dread that women will rise up and assert the power robbed from us? What if it in fact points to a mode of being and presence that is beyond patriarchy's definitions of good and evil? The Antichrist dreaded by the patriarchs may be the surge of consciousness, the spiritual awakening, that can bring us beyond Christolatry into a fuller stage of conscious participation in the 'living' God.

Seen from this perspective the Antichrist and the Second Coming of women are synonymous. This Second Coming is not a return of Christ but a new arrival of female presence, once strong and powerful, but enchained since the dawn of patriarchy.

(Beyond God the Father, P. 96)

Let us ponder for a moment the almost unthinkable radicalism of this feminist thesis. Daly is suggesting we endeavour to see the Antichrist as a liberating force for good in the world and diametrically opposed to the 'divine' Christ who is, in this equation, arguably a major cause of the patriarchal subordination of women... wow! This is pure Tantra! Buddhist Tantra reversed Buddha's anti-erotic teachings and replaced non-desire with desire. Daly wants the same outcome for Christianity. She takes the backbone of Western civilization and breaks it in two with one super-potent sentence: "If God is male then male is God". To expose the world religions for being in the main pseudo-spiritual, even blasphemous instruments of sexist hegemony, would require civilization as we know it to transition through an apocalyptic period of instability. But instead of this happening the feminist 'revolution' seems to have ended, not with a bang but a whimper, attacking soft targets like sex workers and their clients and leaving popes, archbishops, and mullahs largely alone to annoy us with their sanctimonious speeches of peace and reconciliation. Let us look once more at this all important message to women all over the world who seem singularly determined to ignore her to the point of doing the complete opposite and turning down every chance of anything else but tokenism:

As the women's movement begins to have its effect upon the fabric of society, transforming it from patriarchy into something that never existed before... it can become the greatest single challenge to the major religions of the world Western and Eastern. Beliefs and values that have held sway for thousands of years will be questioned as never before. This revolution may well be also the greatest single hope for survival of spiritual consciousness on this planet.
(Beyond God the Father, P. 13)

She wrote that Christianity itself should be 'castrated' by cutting away the products of supermale arrogance: "the myths of sin and salvation that are simply two diverse symptoms of the same disease". Daly shows uncompromising radicalism when she speaks of a new world in *Pure Lust* that will be far more rational when patriarchy, which she calls 'sadosociety', has been overthrown.

If I am allowed to utilise her neologism by making it inclusive of hellfire, which is the real essence of patriarchy, 'sadosociety' becomes the pivotal word to define the geopolitical world we live in where male violence is projected into the sky and instantiated in God. Women have to be helped to understand that there is not a lot of point any longer in simply seeking equality in the sadosociety; they would do better to abolish it. The sadosociety is not going to disappear over night; it may take generations to root out the dark side of religion and warmongering politics, but every journey begins with one step and I believe my art could be that first step, or at least part of that first step, that galvanises the emergence of a new consciousness.

It is well known that countless non-Christians and atheists, many of them heavyweight academics like Bertrand Russell and Richard Dawkins, have expressed their abject horror at the religious doctrine of eternal punishment for the damned. A lesser-known fact is that this aversion to what can only be categorised as religious sadism is shared by millions of Christians. Large numbers of Christians, including Jehovah's Witnesses for example, and many evangelicals and protestant liberals, have already quietly dropped the doctrine of eternal punishment in hell. Even the Catholic Church and the Church of England now try increasingly to distance themselves from this historic love affair with what many seminal academics from all walks of life have denounced as sadomythic nonsense. But what is really notable is that these Christians have not come to this conclusion from scripture initially but from *reason*. This is highly relevant, because believers denouncing each other from a position of faith for heresy or for having false and even blasphemous interpretations of scripture are commonplace, and so subjective that they are meaningless to non-believers. But for religious people to denounce doctrines from reason, from *a priori* objections, is to be taken much more seriously. These Christians simply could not accept the paradox, the anti-logic, of a god of love and justice who inflicted endless physical and mental torments on countless innocents whose only 'crime' was to belong to the 'wrong' religion or none at all.

Let us see this from a woman's perspective, which is highly conscious of issues relating to male violence against women. Half the people sent to hell would be women. Why on earth then do Christian and Muslim women not see that they worship a male-defined sado-God? I hope the reader will just allow me to tidy up my argument here and put the finishing tweaks to my radical thesis, shared to a considerable degree by Mary Daly.

Countless Christians who have rejected hellfire doctrine actually agree with me in thinking that a God of hellfire is a self-contradiction that by definition makes God evil. However, Christians for and against hell have no idea of the far-reaching political implications of their debate. Here I will join up the dots with a little lateral thinking and produce a shocking, even world-shattering, conclusion. Most people, understandably, will be sceptical of attempts by a non-academic like me to turn their world upside down and tell them Western civilization is not based on noble world religions but blasphemy. I beg the reader to stay with me on this tedious, depressing and seemingly unimportant subject. If there is one thing I have learned in all my years on this Godforsaken planet, if there is one unique insight I can lay claim to, it is understanding the spiritual and political implications of this infamous doctrine. This construal is literally the *'dim mak'* or the delayed death touch which when delivered to Islam through radical rationalism will humble it and kill the Islamist beast of doom-laden terrorist rage.

Even though it is unthinkable to most people, it is, as I have said, an idea embraced by millions of Christians themselves, namely that traditional historic Christianity is actually anti-God and insults God by attributing sadistic intentions to him. I will demonstrate this later on in this chapter.

But first I have to recount an important personal anecdote. In my book *Sex and the Devil's Wager* I explain that the Devil's Wager is simply a bet that challenges those who believe in uncritical religious freedom to cite any moral idea by Hitler or any other evildoer that is as evil as the ethic of eternal torture. Believe me, it is impossible to beat this wager, and if it proves, as it does, that the most evil ethic ever invented by the human mind is the central teaching of Christianity and Islam – why do we tolerate them?

Let me give the reader a clue to understanding the significance of the Wager. Firstly I paid three three professional critics to review my book. All of them wrote very unflattering reviews with many quotes taken out of context, but their major failing was to ignore the real subject matter. Not one of them even mentioned the Devil's Wager! This was the title of the book, and the whole reason it exists. If they could have beaten the Devil's Wager, don't you think they would have relished the opportunity? They ignored the Wager because they couldn't beat it. They couldn't beat it because even Hitler didn't want to torture the Jews forever but merely to exterminate them. The holocaust, depraved as it was, is a peccadillo relative to what Jesus intends to do to the same concentration camp victims.

It is a standard theological and historic Christian belief that Jews can't be saved. Millions of Christians today still believe that Jews will never be granted salvation. Jesus, according to Bible teaching, will resurrect the Holocaust victims on Judgement day simply and solely to have them sent to hell to be tortured forever. Simple logic tells us that on this basis alone, Jesus Christ is more evil than Hitler, who put them out of their misery in gas chambers. There are no gas chambers in hell. In hell there is no death - only excruciating punishment. I believe the case for demonstrating that Jesus is more evil than Hitler is actually very strong if you are prepared to think outside the box. But this thesis is unthinkable for a world that would find it almost impossible to adjust to such a revolutionary truth.

After arriving at the sensible conclusion that God by definition cannot be an evil torturer, these anti-hell Christians then turn to scripture in order to re-interpret it to fit their new theology - a theology now based on reason. Therefore evangelicals are basically divided into those who are disgusted by hellfire doctrine and argue that Jesus didn't teach it and those who despite their distaste for the said dogma still feel he did. They have to swallow it whole because they are bound by faith to believe, what in all conscience, they think the Bible teaches, and they then try to justify this position with many spurious arguments. My own view after a lifetime of studying this subject is that the doctrine of hell is evil, but it is nevertheless dominical. Therefore in my book, Jesus Christ is forever contaminated with this horrible dogma and eternally defined by it.

But in order to press home the importance of my Tantric panacea, let me say one more thing before we leave this unsavoury subject to move on to more pleasant pastures. The following quote from a contemporary Christian theologian puts forward a devastating thesis; namely that the historic teaching of both the Catholic Church and the Church of England is virtually satanic!

Let me say at the outset that I consider the concept of hell as endless torment in body and mind an outrageous doctrine, a theological and moral enormity, a bad doctrine of the tradition which needs to be changed. How can Christians possibly project a deity of such cruelty and vindictiveness whose ways include inflicting everlasting torture upon his creatures, however sinful they may have been? Surely a God who would do such a thing is more nearly like Satan than like God, at least by any moral standards, and by the gospel itself.
(*Hell Under Fire*, Clark Pinnock, P.34)

Other theologians go so far as to imply historic Christianity is blasphemous! The world famous Christian theologian and philosopher John Hicks stated that "the idea that God plans to inflict perpetual torture upon any of his children" is beyond belief and even "blasphemous" (*Hell on Trial*, P6).

These frightening admissions from many Christians who regard the conventional concept of God as satanic and blasphemous have somehow not impacted the general public in any way whatsoever, as if they are not the revolutionary political dynamite which they quite obviously are. But this historic version is the very version that the Catholic Church and the Church of England have been teaching for centuries. Is it not worth thinking the unthinkable – that Western civilization is founded on Satanic blasphemy and blasphemy that has propagated fig-leaf phobias about sex and nudity? Am I not justified in being outraged by a world that is more likely to define me as a pornographer and a sexual offender than a spiritually enlightened erotic artist - and yet itself sanctions blasphemy in the hallowed name of uncritical religious freedom? It is the truth that sets you free, not freedom, but freedom is the ultimate sacred cow - the clarion call of freedom-loving America. The love of freedom without the love of truth is a recipe for anarchy. America has never understood this. The French revolution was not just about the love of freedom – it dedicated itself to the love of reason. Reason, rationalism and the love of truth were never an essential part of the American revolution, and now we are all paying the price for this.

The Humanist Margaret Knight is the only female campaigner against hellfire blasphemy I know of, and for this reason I regard her and Mary Daly as leading feminists blazing a path to revolution. Knight was fully cognisant of the need to prioritise awareness of hellfire above any other issue if we are to see Christianity for what it really is. She wrote over forty years ago what all women should be saying and thinking now instead of overstating their concerns about pornography, beauty pageants and prostitution:

The most intolerable of the doctrines taught by Jesus, and the one that has the most hideous social consequences, is the doctrine of hell. This doctrine is still accepted and taught by the Catholic Church, but Christians of other denominations are making desperate attempts to explain it away. But Jesus' statements on the subject are so frequent, and so explicit, that if they are to be dismissed as symbolic or unhistorical it becomes hard to see why any of his reported sayings should be accepted as literally true. (*Honest to Man*, P.37)

She skilfully exposes the duplicitous argument that many modern Christian thinkers use that hell is merely a metaphor for separation from God, brought on by the sinner himself, and goes on to make the valid point that Christianity has double moral standards and is ethically schizophrenic:

Jesus's teaching suggests that different standards apply to our Heavenly Father, who, though by definition all-good and all-loving, will inflict hideous torments throughout eternity on those who displease him, for no motive but vengeance – since there is no possibility of repentance and redemption in hell. The inconsistency is so gross that it simply justifies the description of Christianity as a schizophrenic religion. (P.39)
...a God who consigns anyone, however wicked, to an eternity of agony is a sadistic monster who deserves execration rather than love. (P.40)

She goes on to quote Pope Paul, who in 1971 said 'Hell is a grim reality, even though modern man seems to be losing sight of the frightful danger of eternal doom' (P.168).

Although we are constantly told by politicians and the media that the monstrous barbarism perpetrated by Islamic terrorists has nothing to do with 'real' Islam, informed common sense tells us otherwise, and criticism of religion is intensifying from many diverse perspectives. To excuse Islam, pundits argue that ISIL or Daesh is mainly comprised of political hotheads and not true believers. This is such a misleading argument because it ignores the fact that politics and religion are inseparable in Islam. It also ignores the fact that the history of Daesh is rooted in the serious nuanced theology of many Islamic thinkers and ultimately derives like most terrorist organisations from the Muslim Brotherhood, who after Morsi was deposed, farcically claimed to be defenders of democracy! ISIL's caliphate theology is therefore arguably as authentic an interpretation of Islam as any other.

It is in the nature of monotheism to lend itself to multiple interpretations and versions, none of which have an exclusive claim to being the 'right' one. It is also common in the history of monotheism for different interpreters to denounce each other as heretics. If ISIL is a false interpretation of Islam, where is the corresponding false interpretation of Christianity? Only believers denounce each other as having false interpretations of the holy books. We on the outside rightfully regard all the interpretations of Judaism, Christianity and Islam as equally implausible and equally anti-rational. Hence for non-Muslims there is

Aphrodite

Ardhanari

Kwan Yin

Yab-Yum

Shakti dancing

The author at Angkor Wat

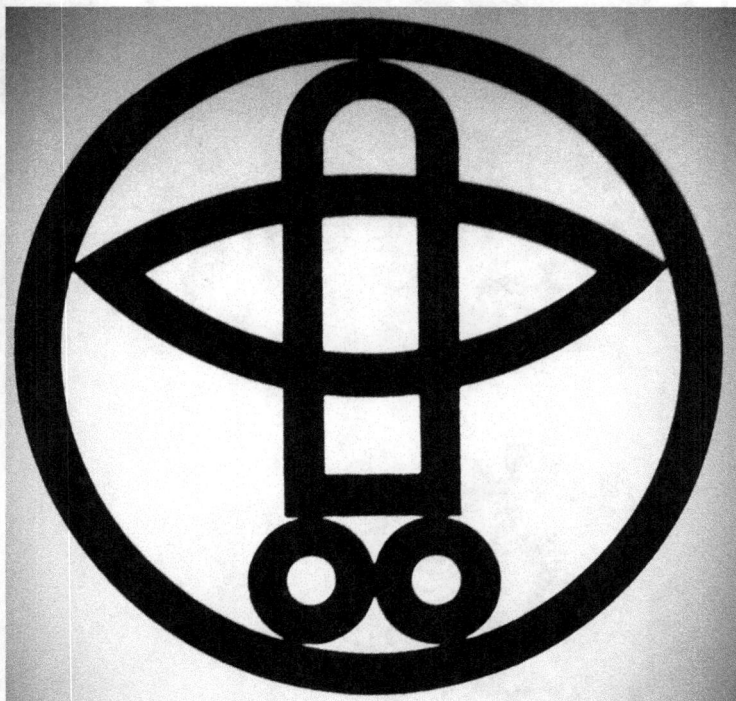

Yoni-lingam logo for Tantric Humanism

Hell Garden in Thailand

Shiva dancing

Yoni-lingam

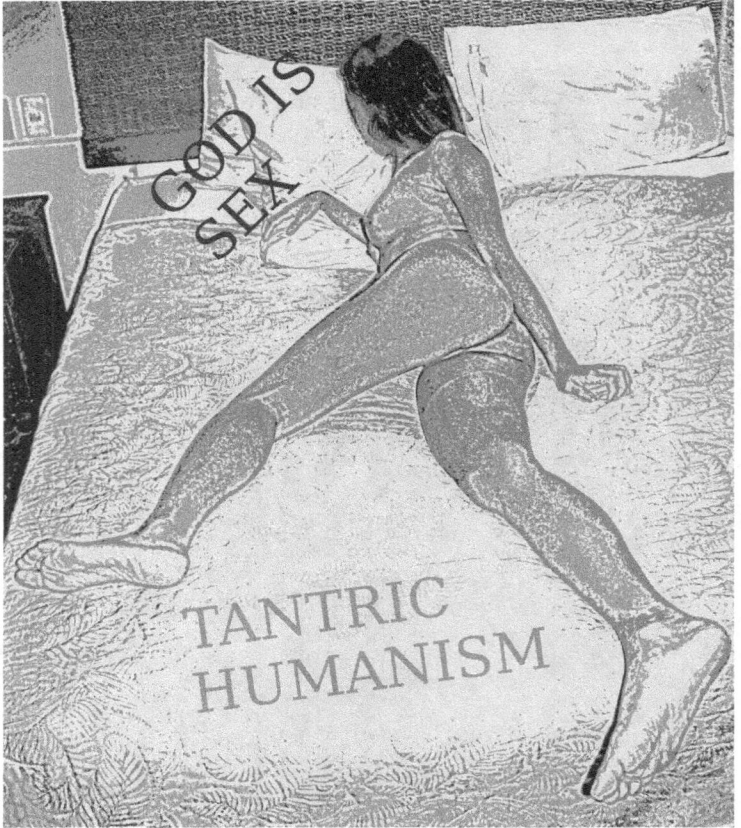

Tantric humanism (poster element)

Hellfire is blasphemy (poster element)

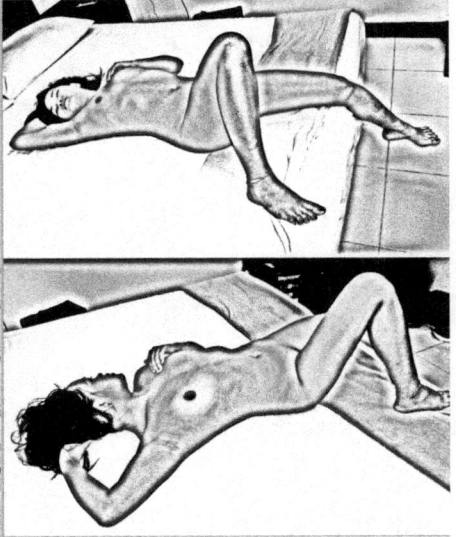

Sex workers are erotic saints (poster element)

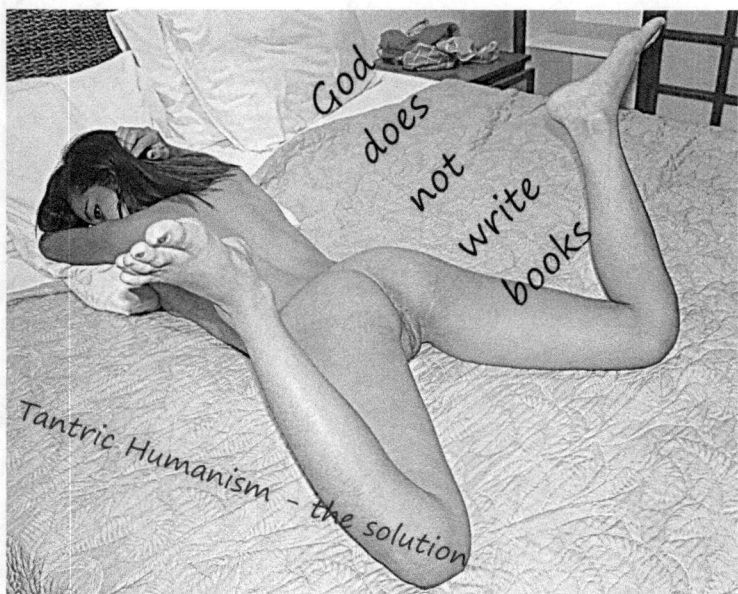

The solution (poster element)

God is dance (poster element)

Flowers of Mongolia (painting)

God is sex – God is Yab-Yum (painting)

Yoni and starburst flower garden (painting)

The dancer (painting)

The third eye (painting)

no demonstrably 'false' interpretation of Islam by sincere believers, and who can doubt the fanatical sincerity of ISIL members? The fact that ISIL is violent is also irrelevant. Islam is not a religion of 'peace and love', as British Muslims keep mendaciously telling us. It has often been historically a religion of war and conquest tempered perhaps with peacemaking periods.

When the Catholic church instigated the Inquisition, which tortured thousands of innocent men and women to death and justified them with scripture, do we say now that they were not true Christians because they acted violently or badly? To ISIL members they are in a total war against the West. It could be argued that ISIL are the true Muslims, as unlike UK Muslims they are not prepared to compromise with 'Western decadence' and want to establish pure Islam uncontaminated with modernism. Western governments cannot admit the truth that violent jihad and Islamist terrorism is a legitimate form of Islam because once the authorities admit this, they have to concede that Islam is in its essence politically toxic and will always be a threat to civilization. In the interests of expediency this is simply unthinkable.

George Orwell famously said that to speak the truth in a time of universal deceit is a revolutionary act . Let us speak this truth out loud: monotheism is a lethal and unacceptable liability in the world today – a cocktail of anti-scientific fallacies. It is presently the underlying cause of virtually every trouble spot on the planet, including Yemen, Afghanistan, Iraq, Israel, Palestine, Syria, Libya and even Tunisia, where the Arab spring first started, and is now having to deal with an Islamist insurgency.

A contentious issue that closely relates to sex and feminism and therefore my artwork is FGM. My paintings are a form of *yoni puja* or vulva worship and the idea of mutilating the vagina is the greatest of profanities. Again political correctness, which may I remind the reader is all about what my art is challenging, gives a completely false narrative to the British people. It is continually claimed by the authorities and Islamic pressure groups that FGM has little or nothing to do with Islam and is in fact merely a cultural custom. The facts however contradict this claim. There is evidence that some Muslim scholars support FGM as a legitimate Islamic custom. Even if you choose not to believe this nonconformist version of the narrative you have to concede the waters are muddied. For a start there is a presumption in Islamic law that what is not prohibited is allowed. FGM is not referred to in the Koran, but why not? The prophet spent plenty of time condemning other things which arguably are far less important, and he knew all about FGM so why doesn't it feature prominently in this book of moral perfection?

One tradition which many Muslims accept as a genuine hadith makes it clear that the prophet supported FGM. Apparently the prophet saw a woman who practised FGM and when he asked her if she still practised it she replied that she did, and would continue to do so as long as he didn't forbid it. He did not however take this opportunity to forbid it but said, "Yes it is allowed but if you cut don't overdo it". Here Muhammad clearly had the opportunity to prohibit it and save the suffering of millions of mutilated women, and he declined. The British people never hear this side of the story from the Muslim propagandists, who it seems to me, get unrestricted access to the media whenever they want it, to reassure the British public that Islam is a perfect religion of peace and devoted to human rights. Some clerics actually say FGM is obligatory and others merely that it is permissible and should not be banned.

I think the evidence suggests that Islam is indeed partly responsible, at the very least, for the mutilation and suffering of millions of women through the centuries. These women would have been saved from this suffering if Muhammed had condemned it as *haram*. Instead he preferred to ban Muslims from having a glass of wine with their dinner. He obviously thought that drinking a glass of wine with your diner was a greater sin than mutilating women's sexual organs. An unfair statement? An Islamophobic rant? I say let us at least debate it, and hopefully without Muslim extremists offering up death threats instead of rational arguments. Is this really too much to ask of a modern democratic society?

Political correctness, especially in the UK, makes it virtually impossible to be heard criticising Islam in public without being immediately damned and gagged as 'Islamophobic', but the definition of a phobia is an irrational aversion or fear of something. How is it that the concept of 'rational aversion' to Islam is never as popular and acceptable to the British media as its beloved 'Islamaphobia'? I believe in the right of citizens in a free society to dislike the belief but not the believer. I have a rational aversion to Islam because it threatens my art and everything I believe in, and it is Islam in my view that is guilty not only of phobias, such as its irrational fear of figurative art, but also an ideology that is anti-scientific and based almost entirely on blind faith.

Let's take the issue of nudity first. The arguments Muslims use to justify covering women's bodies in the name of modesty are in my view self-contradictory and self-defeating, because it doesn't necessarily follow that the more of a woman you conceal the more you respect her for her intellect. If you take concealment and modesty to its logical conclusion (and Muslims do just this) it completely erases a woman, turning a former human being into a genderless anonymous 'thing' under a black tent.

It is argued by Muslim scholars that when women are covered up it frees them from 'sexploitation' and women are not then viewed as sex objects. A typical adherent of these beliefs is Sarah Sheriff, who wrote in a pamphlet I picked up in a Muslim bookshop, *Women's Rights in Islam*, that the Muslim dress code enables the Muslim woman to be seen as 'an intellectual personality' and 'one of the main aims of Islam's dress code is to promote morality in society...'

The clue to the reality behind the dress code and Islam's obsession with modesty lies in the phrase 'promote morality in society'. The real reason for the cover-up is not respect for women but the need to control female sexuality to serve the male fear of hell and damnation. Muslim men don't want to be aroused in public. They are fearful of the primordial urges to commit fornication that a provocatively-clad woman arouses in them. Fornication is forbidden, or 'haram' in Islam, deserving lengthy torture in hell. It is surely a fundamental right of any woman to wear what she likes within the law without having to reference men and ask for their permission or approval. Muslim women who insist that they are exercising that right and choose themselves to wear a religious costume should ask themselves why. Why do they want to wear a costume that symbolises a religion that ratifies the torture of trillions of their non-Muslim sisters in hell? Why do they want to wear a costume which, whether they like it or not, symbolises ISIL and 9/11?

The quite reasonable argument that there is little difference between wearing Nazi regalia and the burka and hijab would not find any traction in our PC media today, suffering as it does from hell-blindness. The Islamic prejudice against Western women's dress codes plays into the notion that women who dress to feel and look sexy are inviting rape, or at least can't complain if they get molested or harassed because they are sending the wrong signals. But this again is based on the idea that men can't be blamed for not controlling their sexual urges and it is not helped by the Islamic disapproval of masturbation, which would help to alleviate any sexual tension from seductive dress codes.

My personal feeling on this is that it's a wonderful thing for women to look sexy because it reminds us of the most beautiful thing in life. But this is all the more reason to legalize prostitution so that this pleasure, in the shape of sexual hospitality, is available to all men on demand from what I describe as willing 'sex and beauty vendors'. I believe that men are quite capable of controlling their libidos even when surrounded by women dressing provocatively, but it is so much more civilised, caring and public-spirited to offer men (and women if they want it) greater access to the joy of sex and the beauty of the naked form that sexy young dressers signify.

The Islamic attitude is also based on the false premise that a woman who arouses lust in a man cannot be respected as a human being at the same time with an equal intelligence to himself. This assumption that men see sexy women as morons is utter nonsense and insulting to men. Only morons see provocatively-dressed women as morons in a post-feminist age. I desire instant sex with every beautiful woman I see without having to know anything about her. I simultaneously have a respect for all women as equals. My male gaze is a perfectly natural attitude for a healthy red blooded heterosexual and is in no way disrespectful to women. It is simply a recognition that sex is for me at least, subjectively speaking, the primal force of the universe and quite literally the life-force of humanity. I strongly resent society trying to make me feel guilty about my wholesome love of women's erotic beauty.

Sheriff uses a further misleading argument when she suggests that men suffer the same restraints in the dress code: "…men are also required by the Qur'an to dress and behave modestly". The flaw in this argument is obviously that men are not asked to cover up nearly to the same extent as women and men's clothes by all tradition are not as revealing in the first place, so the adjustments they have to make for modesty are virtually irrelevant. Added to this, the sexual objectification of men is hardly on an equal level with that of women because men's bodies, according to our cultural traditions, do not have anything like the same effect on women as their own bodies have on men. The sexual objectification of men for women in popular

Western culture is arguably a recent phenomenon and has a long way to go to catch up with the historic ubiquity of the male gaze.

Finally the whole raison d'être of the Muslim argument is shown to be unintelligible when we see the statement taken to its logical conclusion and the dress code allows only the eyes to be seen through the black tent. This is a common sight in many parts of London. Do men look at the Burka tent and say "wow what an intelligent woman?" I don't think so. In fact the woman inside the black tent is arguably negated: in order to obliterate her feminine form the face and the personality are totally and literally blacked out. This I believe is the real objective of the Islamic dress code, namely to silence and then nullify the woman utterly so she ceases to exist. She is dissolved and then reassembled at home where she is allowed to disrobe by male guardians of her virtue where now, hidden from the world, her womanly curves are no longer a threat to male salvation.

Dr. S. Daesh was Imam at the Regents Park Mosque and speaks for basic Islam on matters that directly relate to my art which is not only figurative but 'idolatrous' and erotic and by his values violates everything sacred to Islam. In *Questions and Answers* he states:

At the beginning of Islam, all statues and drawings were prohibited, so that people could concentrate on the reality of the absolute Oneness of Allah, and his transcendence beyond all forms... the Prophet, blessings and peace be upon him, warns very strongly against the depiction of complete human figures, saying that those who draw human figures or animals will be severely punished on the Day of Resurrection... The subject of imagery has divided Muslim scholars for centuries. And the debate on the Islamic validity of art – drawings and paintings – intensified after the invention of the camera, which some scholars campaigned vehemently to ban, saying "Photography is haram for Muslims."' (P. 174-175)

The obscure reasoning for this disturbing phobia against photography, painting and sculpture is "Creation is Allah's domain and it should stay that way" and the fear was, say scholars, "that painting and sculpting might lead people into idol-worship." Daesh insists "there is no justification for any Muslim engaging in sculpture" and he quotes a kosher hadith that says "Allah considers none to be more unjust than those who try to copy His creation."

As is to be expected, other scholars disagree and say this aversion to art was an extreme reaction to idol worship in the early days and can now be more relaxed, but this is no comfort to me or anyone else who believes in artistic freedom. In recent history the Taliban have destroyed priceless archaeological artefacts and sites in Afghanistan, and ISIL have done the same in Iraq and Syria, proving themselves to be typical philistine vandals for the cause of Islam against their historic enemy, namely paganism. As if this isn't enough there are Muslim schools here in Britain that ban photography and tell children it is haram, and there have been vigilante patrols intimidating Londoners claiming they are in a Muslim area where sharia law has to be respected. These Muslim fanatics insulted women who dressed in a Western style and claimed to be on a mission to rid the streets of prostitutes.

Muslims have a history of iconoclasm and vandalism, and the invasion of India from the eighth century onwards resulted in mass slaughter, the enslavement of women and the wilful crass destruction of hundreds, some say thousands, of pagan temples. Certainly hundreds of thousands of idols, apsaras, and erotic sculptures were smashed to pieces. The wrecking of Hindu temples went on for nearly a thousand years, and often mosques were built on the sites of Hindu temple ruins. The Muslims aided the demise of one of the most advanced civilizations on Earth. In its theological purity, Islam is the misogynistic enemy of sexual freedom, free speech, Western figurative art, philosophy and science. The fact that for a relatively short period of time in the history of Islam some Muslims happened to practice science and even make important scientific advances is not in any way evidence that Islam is compatible with science. Islam does not respect learning and knowledge as it claims: it respects learning and knowledge that does not contradict the Koran. A religion that believes in the literal existence of Adam and Eve, heaven and hell, Muhammad's miracles and a host of other lunacies, and follies of faith, is not a religion that respects the supreme authority of scientific knowledge or empiricism!

Islam is based on blind faith: its epistemology is not rationalistic and scientific but it pays a lip service to reason in order to portray itself as a reasonable worldview when it is in fact the complete opposite. It is the epistemological methodology of a religion that defines whether it is compatible with science, not the isolated practice of science by some of the faithful as an epiphenomenon.

Science offers men power, and all men want power, so whatever their religion they will seek knowledge to get it; knowledge is power. This pragmatic attitude doesn't stop them being anti-scientific when their religion demands it. This is how I see it: science and rationalism is my religion as a humanist. During the golden age of Islamic science, Islam, a superstition, used my religion to empower itself with knowledge about medicine etc. This merely proves how inadequate Islam is - that it has to use my religion to fulfil its needs.

The fact that these aforementioned archaic phobias against figural art, photography and music are often ignored by westernised moderate Muslims does not change the fact that they are still there as a submerged menace within Islam and ready to be revived by any radical at any time, as for example in our own times, with the Taliban and ISIL. Islam condemns public nudity, fornication, pornography and prostitution and forbids homosexuality. Daesh reminds his readers that the Koran condemns homosexuality "in the strongest possible terms" (P. 136). Anal sex between heterosexuals is also haram (P114). Segregation of the sexes to minimise temptation is furthermore a strong theme in Islamic teaching, as is its phobia against music. What is thoroughly unacceptable in Islam, he says, is the music of today, which is 'suggestive' or 'erotic' or 'indecent'. Islam, he asserts, disapproves of modern music whose lyrics "describe intimate physical relationships and the beauty of real people" (P.180).

It is also worth mentioning that Daesh makes it clear with a quote from the Koran that however good non-Muslims may be they will not be saved: "And as for anyone who desires a religion other than Islam (submission to Allah), it will not be accepted from him – and in the Hereafter he will be among the losers" (P. 200). This is a fact I know from personal experience that many Muslims themselves do not know. There are many Muslim women, for example, who have told me Mother Theresa will get to Paradise. I'm afraid they are woefully ignorant about their own religion. Apart from anything else, Mother Theresa believed in the Holy Trinity, which is the most unforgivable sin and blasphemy according to the Koran!

To avoid hell, Islam makes it clear you have to be a Muslim, which means accepting that Muhammad is the final prophet from God. Christianity is equally exclusive but insists Jesus is the final prophet. Clearly they can't both be right, and personally I have no doubt whatsoever that they are both wrong!

Buddhism not only condemns prostitution but it arguably forbids sex and procreation, in the sense that it regards both as a barrier to salvation. It has therefore made a regrettable contribution to world sex-phobia. The whole essence of the Buddhist disapproval of sex is bound up with his early life story and his quest for enlightenment. The narrative is well known: Buddha was once a wealthy prince who had several wives and a harem of erotic dancers, but when he realised his golden cage was surrounded by a world full of deceptions and suffering he is reputed to have rejected the love of life and to have come to the conclusion that nothing was more deceptive than a woman's appearance that 'make foolish men mad with desire'. When one realises that women's charms are an illusion, he insisted, men will no longer be deceived.

His lifelong quest then focused on extinguishing the flame of lust and all sexual impulses so that a naked woman dancing before him would leave him utterly unmoved, and he achieved this when he passed his final test from Mara, the evil one, who sent a bevy of beautiful seductive goddesses dancing and gyrating around him in various states of undress and inviting him to unimaginable sexual delights, but Buddha calmly ignored them.

One of Buddha's earliest discourses was the Fire Sermon in which he rightly recognised the sex drive as the most powerful life force, keeping us on the wheel of earthly existence – the blaze of passion is the primary element of the will to live and the thirst that keeps the wheel of life spinning faster. In an inverted sense, Buddhism, like most religions, actually attests to and pays homage to the peerless power of sex and the seductive charisma of prostitutes and erotic dancers by regarding them as the greatest threat to its principles and practices. Buddha saw sex as a negative and destructive force that increased the appetite for life and procreation. He is reputed to have said that it is better for a man to put his penis in the mouth of a cobra than into a vagina.

To "cure" such addiction to the pleasures of the flesh, Buddhist texts prescribe a number of remedies, the most effective being meditation on the loathsomeness of the body and recognition that beautiful women are in essence "nothing more than bags of skin filled with blood, pus, and filth." The loveliest woman is, he pointed out, destined to turn into an ugly old crone and then just worm food in the dirt. In Buddhism the seductive feminine form is the ultimate temptation to spiritual regression or to the

Buddhist version of sin. She is the most powerful threat to liberation that the male monk faces.

In Tantric Buddhism this narrative is completely reversed, but common to both perspectives is the mutual acknowledgement of the exalted status of the feminine body and its transformative power over the male psyche. There is a Buddhist story that a monk was once confronted by a gorgeous stripper. After she removed her clothes he demanded she take off her skin! The significance being of course that underneath the skin there is an asexual anatomical inner body, which is a very sobering thought for the voyeur when he becomes mindful of the blood and bones that lie hidden beneath the bewitching surface. One of the favourite ploys of Mara, the Evil One, was to transform himself into a stunning beauty whenever Buddha addressed a crowd of men.

I hope I am slowly building up a convincing case for my central argument here that the real reason the stripper is feared and maligned by all religions is because she is actually the most powerful signifier of the one true religion, namely natural religion or Pantheism, and this is what feminists have arguably failed to fully understand. Feminism is partially blinded by its own rhetoric on this matter, because men in the past have used the idea of woman as 'Nature' to belittle her intellect through the patriarchal dualism of male as objective science versus female as subjective nature.

Many Buddhist texts are extremely misogynistic and insulting to women. Women represent sex and childbirth, and if Buddhism is taken literally it wants to end sex and procreation. Admittedly Buddha only prescribed celibacy for priests and those that could handle it, but the fact remains that like Jesus who praised eunuchs, his teachings are anti-erotic and arguably a kind of death cult which pictures life as a wheel of woe and inescapable suffering. If abstaining from sex is the insignia of enlightenment and enlightenment should be the goal of all human beings, it follows that people seeking liberation are going to have a negative attitude to sex. Good moral ideas should be able to be applied universally, but if everybody became a Buddhist priest the human race would die out.

John Stevens, referencing Buddha's Fire Sermon states:

Sex, "the blaze of passion," is the primary element of the will to live and the chief expression of craving, the "thirst" that creates the chaos, unease, and suffering that plagues the world. More than anything else, it is the cords of sensuous desire that bind us tighter and tighter to the wheel of life – contact, symbolized by a couple in sexual congress, is the middle link in Buddha's twelve-linked "chain of dependent origin." Sex is a raging fire that scorches and burns, flaring up with intense heat, engulfing the scaffold of self-control and restraint that leads to deliverance. (Lust for Enlightenment, P.22)

In Tantric Buddhism, which is virtually a reverse image of orthodox Buddhism, Buddhahood is said to reside in the female sex organs and women are venerated as the 'Great Symbol of Enlightenment'. Woman is the embodiment of Nature and is envisaged as a cosmic mandala. A mandala is a meditative diagram of the universe. Admittedly this Great Symbol is usually a nubile sexually-alluring representative of the female gender and this reverence is male-specific but all the religions of the world are designed *by* men and *for* men, so this is hardly surprising. What I'm concerned with is that out of all the male-defined religions, Tantra is the best religion for moving us towards a unisex pantheism or natural religion that can eventually accommodate all women's needs as equals.

The twenty-first century, in my view, gives us an unprecedented opportunity for the first time in the history of mankind to celebrate human sexuality as it truly should be celebrated. The scientific understanding of genetics and procreation is a recent phenomenon that past pagan cultures that celebrated sex in religion and art had no real understanding of. I can only imagine the incredible sex temples we could build now, surpassing the erotic Indian Temples of Konarak and Khajuraho, if Christianity were replaced with Tantric paganism as our national religion. I dream of cathedrals of joy reaching to the clouds in homage to the nude form and human procreation. I postulate that this pagan revolution cannot happen without the feminist 'Kali' Antichrist.

Feminism is tasked with a major role as perhaps the principle revolutionary catalyst, but in order for this to happen the feminist movement needs to completely change its priorities. It needs to embrace bi-gender sexual objectification and the legalisation of prostitution, and above all it needs to call for hellfire theology to be morally condemned and this condemnation to be enshrined in a revised version of the Universal Declaration of Human Rights. But if Kali is the warrior aspect of feminism, then the goddess Kwan Yin is its loving heart. Aphrodite is the whore element of the feminist Antichrist – the brazen hooker and the sexually-independent woman who fucks who she wants when she wants without giving a thought to her critics. Kwan Yin is about love, compassion and virtue. She is said to be the goddess who 'hears the cries of the world', and is sometime depicted with a thousand arms to maximise her help to others in need.

Her great claim to fame in my view is her unique ability to change the flames of hell to flowers. She was sent to hell, but her virtuous presence set many souls free and it was turned into a paradise by her feminine charisma. She had to be expelled by the Lord of Hell in order for hell to continue its tortures without interruption! This is obviously of major symbolic importance for me, and she is one of the deities that feature in my artwork alongside Kali and Aphrodite. Kwan Yin, unlike Jesus, is the real deity of mercy who feels the pain of human sorrow. Muslim and Christian women should come to their senses and ask themselves what is meant by 'Jesus the Lamb of God' and 'Allah the merciful' when they both want to fan the flames of hell while Kwan Yin turns them into roses and lotus blossoms. Am I still allowed to speak the truth in my own country that prides itself on free speech? Am I allowed to tell the truth, that based on a lifetime of autodidactic research, I have come to the conclusion that it is fair to define Christian and Muslim women as metaphysical bimbos suffering from hell-blindness? I say this for their own good – it's called tough love; a good robust, justified insult can sometimes wake people up and produce beneficial results. The truth is there to offend.

CHAPTER THREE

Jesus – the friend of prostitutes?

It is just another myth of our times that gives the Jesus of the New Testament the credit for being the friend, almost the patron saint, of prostitutes. He didn't say to sex workers that they should carry on doing the good work. Instead, association with them was based on his desire to persuade them to repent. Since fornication is a sin deserving damnation and prostitution is the prime example of fornication, we can assume that Jesus, the friend of prostitutes, would eventually send those who did not repent to hell to be systematically tortured in the style of the Inquisition, no doubt!

Some of the theological giants of Christianity have expressed extreme hostility to prostitutes. St Augustine also considered women to be inferior to men, for only men were fully created in the image of God. He accepted prostitution as a necessary evil which should be tolerated to keep 'honourable' women and girls safe from male lust. St John Chrysostom taught that sex was a bad consequence of Adam and Eve's disobedience. Martin Luther condemned all sex outside marriage, including prostitution, calling prostitutes "stinking... tools of the devil.' Thomas Aquinas agreed with Augustine that prostitution was a safety valve but nevertheless a 'lawful immorality'.

Unfortunately in many countries today even this risible paradox of a lawful immorality is not acceptable. Instead we have a worse 'solution' to the problem. The sad attitude that now prevails in many sex hotspots today from Hong Kong and Thailand to the Philippines is that of turning a blind eye to unlawful immorality. "It's immoral and illegal but we'll tolerate it because it makes money", says Big Brother graciously.

The witchcraze of the Inquisition is well known to all, but let us not forget this had a lot to do with religion's twisted views about sex and fictitious fantasies about sex orgies with the devil. The authors of the *Malleus Malifacarum* were obsessed with sex and believed sex was the reason women were witches which is why they stated:

All witchcraft comes from carnal lust, which in women is insatiable... Wherefore for the sake of fulfilling their lusts they (women) consort with devils.

Tertullian said of women:
You are the devil's gateway... How easily you destroyed man, the image of God. Because of the death which you brought upon us, even the Son of God had to die.

With the collapse of Rome, the Christian church specifically identified the whore with the evil lusts of the flesh, based on the Old Testament and St Paul's misogyny. It was partly through the teachings of St Augustine on prostitution that the church often tolerated priests having concubines. During the crusades of the early Middle Ages thousands of whores made the journey to the Holy Land with the Christian armies. Alongside the church's pimping it paradoxically ran conversion programmes for repentant whores. Around the 13th century, popes exhorted all good Christians to reclaim whores, but throughout Christendom there was widespread sexual hypocrisy and popes, bishops, clergy, kings and princes used whores on a regular basis.

The church itself was the biggest pimp and held the major economic interest in the medieval sex industry, both as landlords and through more direct exploitation. The Church's ownership of whorehouses was rife at times and even the papacy owned brothels and many of them in London. So successful were the Church's brothels that their income helped finance its building programme throughout the entire Middle Ages, and many of London's churches were built on the proceeds of prostitution.

The Puritan movement was personified by the 17th century Puritan ideologue William Stubbs, who denigrated dance as a preparation for wantonness and lewdness and "an introduction to whoredom". To Stubbs, there was "no greater sin before the face of God than whoredom" and he listed a long litany of risible health risks including premature ageing, memory loss and last but not least "everlasting damnation".

Christianity has shown through the centuries complete hypocrisy in its stance on prostitution. There should have been zero tolerance of this Christian vice if the Church was to be faithful to its founder. Theories about a different New Age Jesus who married and had children are irrelevant to the issue I raise here, which is about determining the effect of Christ's anti-erotic influence on history up to our own times. It is the Jesus of the Bible and of the Church teaching that is the Jesus who has actualised the skewed culture I now live in, where genitals are still taboo and shameful and often gratuitously censored.

I don't want to turn the world into a vast nudist camp. A love of nudism does not mean indiscriminate public nudity with no restrictions, but the fact is we don't at present have any positive message about nakedness and nudity to offer the younger generation. Some try to argue that Jesus wasn't puritanical and they blame St Paul for Christianity's terrible fig leaf legacy, but in fact he has made his own contribution to the world's sex phobia because, as I've pointed out already, he strongly condemned the male gaze as a form of mental adultery and fornication. We can safely assume on this basis that he would have emphatically condemned even soft pornography and erotic imagery of any kind. We can also assume from his general Judaic orthodoxy on sexual matters that he would have almost certainly disapproved of homosexuality.

His puritanism was commented on by Margaret Knight:

His attitude to sexual love was consistent with his attitude to family affection and family ties in general – that his followers should avoid them as far as possible, since they tended to interfere with an exclusive devotion to God. Thus he spoke with apparent approval of those who have 'made themselves eunuchs for the kingdom of heaven's sake' (Matt. 6:12) and assured his disciples there would be no marriage in the world to come...
(Honest to Man, P. 43)

It is perhaps worth noting that whereas Jesus said there is no sex in heaven (because we can surely assume if there is no marriage there will be no sex unless claimed otherwise) the teachings of Islam are the opposite, promising a sex orgy in paradise – at least for men! Any village idiot should be able to work out that at least one of these afterlife scenarios must be wrong, and personally I wouldn't give either of them a dollar's worth of credibility. It must also be remembered that European colonialism was a Christian evangelistic propaganda machine of forced conversion that was guilty of some of the worst acts of violence and injustice ever committed against humanity. These were perpetrated in the name of Jesus Christ and justified by biblical texts. The American holocaust, which began in the fifteenth century, was supported by popes and archbishops and droves of complicit participating priests who witnessed first-hand the monstrous atrocities and often blessed the savagery and brutality that destroyed hundreds of disparate pagan cultures.

Generations of genocidal Christian sadists enslaved and butchered to death millions of men, women and children for gold and greed. With the help of what they believed was God-sent smallpox and other devastating diseases formerly unknown to the victims, they slaughtered and tortured to death nearly one hundred million members of the indigenous pagan populations of the Americas. The Nazi holocaust pales into insignificance alongside this abomination. In 2015 Pope Francis, on a visit to South America, apologized for the crimes of the Church in this part of the world, which has never fully recovered and still bears the scars and long-term effects of its ruination for the sake of gold, slaves, profit and Jesus Christ.

These same colonialists nevertheless assumed the moral high ground over whores, and never missed an opportunity to slander them for their victimless crimes serving male concupiscence. After decimating the population of much of South America, the Christian establishment imposed its church courts that were hell-bent on stamping out sexual misconduct which in their twisted outlook even involved dance, and as a consequence public dance was for periods banned. A Mexican priest's tirade against harlots typified attitudes in Latin America at this time when he called them "dancers of the devil, scandalous persons" and "nets of the devil, basilisks of the streets and windows" who killed with their "stirrings".

Converts had the good fortune of being introduced to the Catholic practice of confession and penance that invaded the private spaces of the soul and required a body to be denied masturbatory relief and a mind purged of all unauthorised sexual thoughts. Everywhere the Catholic priests and Protestant hellfire preachers went they spread the same intolerant sex ethic. Religious and civic leaders increasingly regarded prostitutes as worse than other criminals, for they seduced other citizens from the life of moral order that authorities regarded as essential to a godly city. Women charged with prostitution were usually so poor that punishment by fine was impossible, so they were imprisoned, punished corporally and then banished, and by the seventeenth century in England this banishment could include deportation. Repeat offenders were sometimes executed.

In India, British Christian colonialism combined with puritanical Indian nationalism to almost destroy one of the greatest dancing traditions in the history of the world. Since the 16th century devadasis had functioned as both courtesans and secular dance artists and their lifestyle was eventually criminalized on the basis of their non-conjugal sexuality, which was seen as prostitution. The Madras Devadasis Act of 1947 outlawed their practices and made it illegal to dedicate devadasis to the temple. They were also called 'nautch girls'. The anti-nautch movement was protesting against the salon dancing more than temple dancing because it was often erotic and performed in private residences of the social elite. The Tawaif were also courtesans who served nobility and excelled in dance and music. The rise of Christian fundamentalism in the UK and especially the fanatical prudery of the Social Purity Movement led to the anti-nautch campaign.

The missionaries in India called upon the British to boycott devadasis and not to attend functions where they performed. The devadasis were demonised by Christians and described by them as hideous creatures with 'hell in their eyes and in their breasts oceans of poison'. Round their comely waists, it was said, dwelt 'the furies of hell' and their smiles were 'India's death'. As their dance skills were less in demand they turned more to prostitution and became a dying breed, but their skills were partly saved by the 'passing of the torch', whereby some of the skills were passed on to non-erotic entertainers and professional dancers.

The Christians tried to marry the devadasis off and make them more respectable, but their dancing was criminalised and dancing became unlawful. This was typical of the sex censors, whether they are religious bigots or anti-porn feminists - they always throw the baby out with the bath water instead of isolating the cancer and making a surgical strike. Therefore instead of focusing on abuse of minors in the devadasi system they tried to get rid of the whole thing and destroyed a priceless dance tradition.

Mahatma Gandhi, who was ashamed of India's celebrated erotic temples, was of course disapproving of the devadasi practice and called for men to be shamed for using them. This great hero of peaceful protest was in my view a narrow-minded prude, and from a Tantric perspective, better defined as spiritually retarded with his deep respect for Jesus Christ the hellfire preacher and his profound support for erotic censorship. He hated the historic sex temples of Konarak and Khajuraho. He felt repulsed by devadasis and regarded their voices against the abolitionists as unworthy of attention, arrogantly asserting that their opinions counted no more than 'keepers of opium dens'. He called for them to give up their sinful ways and take up spinning and weaving for a living, admitting their income could never match what they got through dancing. Some devadasis continued to dance even under the ban and prosecutions failed, because the law only prohibited dancers in temples or religious ceremonies and these dancers performed at social functions. The rehabilitation of devadasis was a social catastrophe and just ruined the lives of thousands of artists and musicians. The hate campaign against devadasis stigmatised them further in the community and opened them up to ridicule for shaming Hindu culture. Many lost wealth and land and large numbers were bribed by missionaries to convert to Christianity because accepting conversion entitled them to financial support.

The anti-nautch movement desired the abolition of dedicating girls to the temple. Hindu nationalism was born in a new guise of prudery that turned against the devadasi tradition it had itself created in more enlightened times. Missionaries called on the British colonialist to stop hiring nautch girls and to boycott erotic dancing. The Hindu reformers of the late nineteenth century were disturbed by the fact that the devadasi institution provided religious sanction for prostitution. They used the devadasi as a way to reform Hinduism and to express condemnation of public immorality and eventually with the help of missionaries persuaded British courts to have devadasis legally declared prostitutes. They were seen as a threat to the reputation of the Hindu religion, and many of their wonderful dance traditions were lost forever.

It is no mere coincidence that monotheism, especially

Christianity and Islam, have historically had a very negative attitude to any form of dance that exhibits the feminine form seductively, and today Islam imposes Draconian restrictions and penalties on women's public dancing in many parts of the world. I believe the underlying reason for this fear of the erotic dancer is that she is in fact a primal subliminal messenger – a signifier who is signalling an invitation to embrace paganism and Natural Religion. This in turn opens the door to pantheism, which is the natural antagonist of monotheism. I believe that when men see erotic dancing, they feel hints of deep, repressed atavistic stirrings welling up from their subconscious – pagan vestiges of nature worship and distant echoes of the mother goddess. I wonder if anybody has realised this truth yet? I wonder if any of the great academic sexologists have actually grasped what the sadosociety really fears about strippers? The erotic dancer reminds men and women of their Shiva/Shakti essence, which has been overlaid with a thick patina of monotheistic body phobia. At a deep subconscious level the stripper is the call of the wild, calling us to embrace Mother Nature and to adopt Natural Religion where women are equal powerholders. The go-go dancer reminds us of sun and moon worship, and pagan standing stones and long-lost sex rituals. She tells us simply with the rhythm of her body to reject the male sadogods of hellfire and damnation.

CHAPTER FOUR

The Case For Prostitution

I am not attempting here to give an exhaustive academic dissertation on all the arguments for and against prostitution, merely to add some elements to strengthen the position I have already taken in previous chapters on this issue. What needs to be understood is that religion and feminism have converged in our times to demonise prostitution with a new vehemence. Traditionally religion defines sex outside marriage as fornication and a sin. Prostitution is arguably the most blatant and emphatic form of fornication. Feminism has introduced sexual objectification into the debate and prostitution is seen as its most blatant form, in which women are said to be reduced to their bodies and more specifically their sexual organs. So we have the conflation of these two narratives, which I hope to deconstruct and prove to be dangerously misleading.

Sexual objectification in its worst form was definitely at the heart of the comfort women scandal, one of the most appalling examples of forced prostitution, which was carried out by Japan in World War II. As many as 200,000 women, commonly called 'comfort women', were forced into prostitution, brutally beaten, raped and held prisoner throughout Asia under the direct control of the Japanese military. State-sanctioned brothels operated virtually wherever there were Japanese troops. The comfort women who were forced to work as sex slaves in these brothels came from Korea, Japan, Indonesia, China, the Philippines and the Netherlands. I have never denied there is a very dark side to prostitution which reflects the daemonic side of male sexuality – a sexual profile that includes rape, violence and multiple forms of historic persecution and abuse of women as a gender underclass. My argument is simply that this narrative should not be used as a pretext to abolish prostitution itself when there is arguably nothing wrong in principle with the sale of sexual services between consenting adults. I believe that the model of prostitution that we find in Angeles City and Pattaya, albeit far from perfect, is a good starting point for establishing a case for prostitution as a social plus for any civilised society that is prepared to liberate itself from the dangerous vestiges of historic religious puritanism that still muddy the waters of human sexuality.

We also need to ask ourselves why sexual objectification is seemingly a male-specific trait that directly relates to male sexuality and if this is so, should men try to change the male gaze or defend it? I believe the male gaze is not a social construct but a natural sexo-aesthetic response to the beauty of the feminine body and should therefore be better understood and defended.

My basic position then is that in the present anti-erotic global culture that prevails, religion and feminism are unwittingly working in tandem for similar goals, despite a dissimilar rhetoric. We are in grave danger of throwing the baby out with the bath water. Those who want to abolish prostitution see it wrongly, in my view, as one of a plethora of immoral and unlawful acts associated with the dark side of human sexuality such as sex trafficking, rape and violence against women. Consensual prostitution, defined as sexual transactions between informed adults for their mutual benefit, is a fundamental social good and arguably a necessary part of what constitutes civilization, and it has to be separated from the dross. The problem is that this fact is lost in the misogynistic sexual chaos of our times where there is still a global climate of rape, child marriage, FGM, sex trafficking, domestic violence, cyber abuse of minors and paedophilia. It is this global climate of women-hating abuse that needs to be understood, and let me suggest that religion must take some of the blame.

It certainly didn't help when men first started to suffer the delusion that they could translate the mind of God and therefore own the divine mandate to control women. Rape and the capture of your enemy's women as sex slaves fits perfectly with the metaphysical psychology of men seeing themselves as hegemonic and superior to women. The idea that God is merely a self-projection of men into the sky has been posited by many seminal minds including the highly influential 19th century philosopher Ludwig Feuerbach. He famously said that religion is man-made and theology is anthropology, and this insight was later upheld by Sigmund Freud. They both defined religion as wishful thinking whereby men have projected their own egos into the sky and named that projection 'God', after which they conveniently got revelations from their own self-projection and gave themselves divine authority for their stupid theobabble.

I have some unique insights into prostitution that you can only learn by using sex workers in the field. I have paid for sex with hundreds of hookers of almost every nationality and I have had lasting relationships with some of them, which have given me valuable revelations about their everyday lives as prostitutes. What follows is a personal testament outlining some of the issues and misunderstandings that I feel are preventing overdue reforms.

We need to decriminalise and destigmatise the act of buying and selling sexual services when it is a voluntary act of mutual benefit between adults. How is it that we have come to be sexually liberal as far as gay sex is concerned and so illiberal towards prostitution? I use 'femprude' in this chapter as a derogatory term to characterise those particular feminists I regard as my opponents; this appellation simply means that in my estimation these women represent an anti-erotic worldview that is founded on prejudice and patriarchal delusions that they have unwittingly internalised and sadly made their own.

I believe the right to buy and sell sexual services is not only morally acceptable but morally desirable, and should be seen in its highest mode as one of the defining principles of civilization. Prostitution is the social recognition of the Tantric principle, which is also a rational principle, that sex is about a whole package of important human needs and ultimately honours the life force. Its availability to all citizens should be facilitated, not hindered, by the State. For me, the idea that prostitution by definition is sexual abuse or mutually demeaning is wrong, and the immemorial stigmatisation of prostitution and the modern crackdown on it in many parts of the world is a retrogressive step and a gross violation of human rights.

The anti-erotic feminist Susan Brownmiller argued that it should be a criminal act to purchase another's body. She paralleled the Christian attitude that wanted sex workers to be rehabilitated by Christian awareness with her own view, that they need rehabilitation through 'feminist' consciousness-raising. Is there such a thing as free and voluntary prostitution? No, she said, along with other campaigners like her, because all prostitution by definition is abuse and is therefore forced. Prostitutes who claim they are there for consent are duped by patriarchal values and can't recognise their own oppression.

How patronising and sexist this attitude is. One could hardly find a greater irony than pompous academics posing as feminists infantilizing women in the sex trade as mindless victims who are not as intelligent and rational as themselves. They are constantly trying to dumb down sex workers and the millions of normal intelligent women who sell some kind of sexual service to men. Is this feminism? I thought feminism was supposed to be based on respect for women, not contempt for the millions of decent human beings in the sex trade who make informed choices and are simply making the best of a selfish capitalist market run largely by banksters. Non-trafficked voluntary sex workers don't want to be rehabilitated and it disempowers them when others see them as victims. It also stigmatises them, thereby making their work far more difficult. If customers see feminists bad-mouthing sex workers, how can we expect them to show the girls respect? Lack of respect for prostitutes from customers is already a serious problem and femprudes only exacerbate it. It is the femprudes who can't recognise their own oppression through internalising patriarchal prejudices.

I think a good place to start would be to analyse the radical heterophobic and misandrist propaganda of Andrea Dworkin, for one very good reason. She regards all heterosexual intercourse as demeaning to women, and if I am interpreting her rant correctly she sees very little difference, if any, between sex with a prostitute and sex with a wife or girlfriend, since they all meet at the same place, namely the subordination of women by men. So here we have the basic sexual act being subjected to the ruthless scrutiny of a lesbian extremist. It doesn't get more black and white than this. I regard intercourse as a sacrament that should form the basis of a new state religion, and she regards it as an act of misogyny that hopefully will die out altogether, since it is immoral and no longer necessary to procreation!

Dworkin was arguably a misandrist, lesbian heterophobe. She certainly regarded heterosexual sex per se as the root of women's subordination, reinforcing men's violent behaviour. Sex becomes defined by the male as sexual colonization, because men want to own or possess women. The penis is a symbol of terror, and heterosexual sex is violence against women. The vehicle used by the male colonizers to exercise their domination over their female territories is pornography. The women represented in pornographic pictures are 'objects' and the photographer or writer is an 'aggressor'. Porn doesn't just cause violence against women, in her view it is violence in itself: porn is the theory, rape is the practice. Pornography depicts women as whores.

In her diatribe against heterosexuality from her book 'Intercourse', she wrote that men hate the vagina and have a 'goose-stepping hatred of cunt'. All the following quotes are from this book. I think her anti-male propaganda is courageous yet jaundiced and at times seriously flawed. I love her anti-establishment militancy but despise her ideas.

She claims men fundamentally hate the vagina despite any highfalutin rhetoric they might employ to hide the fact. They find it physically dirty and foul smelling and it symbolises women who they resent because of the power they hold over them as the withholders of sex.

For the male, the repulsion is sexually intense, genitally focused, sexually solipsistic, without any critical or moral self-consciousness. (Intercourse, p. 9)

I believe there is some truth in this. I myself have heard leery louts joke about fishy-smelling vaginas. Many men are childish and disrespectful to women's bodies, especially when they are drunk and out with the lads. The group mentality brings out the worst in men. Yet despite the fact that far too many men still have crude and slanderous attitudes to women, especially prostitutes, I feel attitudes are improving. I don't believe the average well-educated, post-feminist male thinks this way about women or the vagina.

It may also be true that men have a deep unconscious resentment of the power women have to withhold their bodies from them. I can only speak for myself. I certainly feel this resentment very strongly, but it is not directed at women themselves but at the necessary rules of both society and nature. In my Freudian id I want immediate access to the body of every woman I find fanciable, but my conscience quite rightly tells me this is for very good reasons impossible. Nevertheless this intense vexation and frustration remains like a dark cloud in my soul, directed not at women but at fate, in much the same way as death and the fear of death festers like a paranoid cancer in my brain.

Men, said Dworkin, are always lying about high sentiments but "really only want her body" and resent the power women have over them. They hate the way women own their own bodies. Intercourse is a form of possession or an act by which a man "inhabits" a woman and "occupies and rules over her". In intercourse the woman is a "space inhabited"... "a literal territory occupied literally".

I have to admit that my quest for sex with multiple bar girls is based on the quest for possession of their bodies. I have to penetrate them because I need to fuse with them to become one. But my desire to possess is not to disrespect or harm them but to join and to overcome duality. I need to merge with my other half. For me the possession is part and parcel of a much bigger experience of oceanic oneness with the Other – the lost Other. But Dworkin would have dismissed this as pseudo-metaphysical subterfuge hiding my real motives:

He has her, or, when he is done, he has had her. By thrusting into her, he takes her over. His thrusting into her is taken to be her capitulation to him as a conqueror; it is a physical surrender of herself to him; he occupies and rules her, expresses his elemental dominance over her, by his possession of her in the fuck... The normal fuck by a normal man is taken to be an act of invasion and ownership undertaken in a mode of predation; colonializing, forceful (manly) or nearly violent; the sexual act that by its nature makes her his. (Intercourse. P 73)

I don't believe I have to carry the sexist baggage of others round my neck like a rotting albatross. I am not an embodiment of historical patriarchy, so when I have sex with a woman I am an individual, and so is she. It is true each sex worker is an archetypal representative of all the women I desire – she is Aphrodite, and in this sense she is a generic template, but she is also idiosyncratic in mind, body and soul and these variables are what make the whole quest exciting. But Dworkin would have none of this, as the following quote shows:

Intimate, raw, total, the experience of sexual possession for women is real and literal, without any magical or mystical dimension to it: getting fucked and being owned are inseparably the same; together, being one and the same, they are sex for women under male dominance as a social system. In the fuck, the man expresses the geography of his dominance: her sex, her insides are part of his domain as male... Most women are not distinct, private individuals to most men; and so the fuck tends towards the class assertion of dominance. (Intercourse. P.76)

At other times in her book she went further and argued that even in a society where sexual equality exists, heterosexual intercourse would still be intrinsically an expression of sexual inequality because of the nature of the act - "entry, penetration, occupation... The woman cannot forcibly penetrate the man".

No metaphysical or visionary ideology can reform or redeem intercourse, which of course rules out any Tantric spirituality which she would dismiss as humbug were she to be asked no doubt.

In it, the female is bottom, stigmatized. Intercourse remains a means or the means of physiologically making a woman inferior... (Intercourse, P. 162)

She ridicules the view of elemental gender principles which I hold dear as a Tantric datum.

Both conceptual systems – the theological and the biological – are loyal to the creed of male dominance and maintain that intercourse is the elemental (not socialized) expression of male and female, which in turn are the elemental (not socialised) essences of men and women. (Intercourse, P.73)

Intercourse, Dworkin said, enchains women as it divides them and sex with prostitutes keeps them incarcerated in a ghetto of sexual subservience while the "legal fuck" keeps the wife used, controlled and sexually subservient in the home. The final nail in the coffin? Intercourse is obsolescent and "not necessary to existence any more" because of new reproductive technologies. This is a radical lesbian's point of view, so I would like to counter this assault on heterosexuality and natural procreation. If my art celebrates heterosexual sex as it does, and if I am prescribing a social metaphysic based on the Tantric aesthetic of yin and yang and yoni-lingam dualism I need to say why I think the state celebration of male/female sex and the beauty of heterosexual procreation is valid.

Dworkin was right to say there is a predatory element in male sexuality and that it is related to occupation and possession, and for some retarded men unfortunately it's about dominance, but I don't think sexual possession has to be sexist. I am a hunter, and I even admit to being a 'lustful prowler', to use an erstwhile feminist phrase, but I am not a harmer, and the possession I experience is a mental possession. The actual physical act is more like a visitation. When pilgrims visit a holy shrine they enter the sanctum sanctorum and feel blessed, and when they return they have a possession in the form of a memory. I enter the body of a woman as if it's a temple and this is my visitation. Afterwards I 'possess' her in the form of a memory, vitally enhanced with photographs, mental images and recollections. I also possess time. This is the most important element. I have her body hopefully in its prime and frozen in time. She doesn't grow old and she never refuses my votive voyeuristic gaze. If this is possession then *mea culpa*, and I see nothing wrong with it.

I think it is also important to consider the woman's feelings on this matter. Does the sex worker feel possessed and degraded in the sense that Dworkin means it? This is a woman who has learned to have detached sex when she wants it to be that way and to enjoy it when it suits her, and believe me some of them do enjoy it even with senior citizens! I doubt very much if she feels possessed by a man who means little to her except money and is gone from her life for ever after an hour or two. As for photographs, I'm sure her concerns are not with men who keep them as private possessions or paint pictures from them, but only for men who publish them hurtfully through the social media.

For the sex worker I'm sure there is a big difference between voluntarily selling a sexual service for money and getting raped. But Dworkin might arguably see them as equally demeaning to women. Dworkin's rant relates more accurately to criminals kidnapping women as sex slaves, but I am given permission for my possession, which is therefore bilateral and is not about controlling women in any real sense at all.

A brief encounter with a woman who allows me to document her beauty to be transmuted later into art for posterity is not about hurting women but celebrating their comeliness and their gentleness and their non-violence. My possession of a woman's body is never ownership or political control: I simply prostrate myself inside the temple in gratitude and awe, and leave. Deep in my soul I have a visceral need to merge with them or to metaphysically absorb them into my being, and this only strengthens my respect for the core Tantric myth that God splits into male and female and is forever seeking to merge and re-unite. I am subjectively Shiva seeking to become one with Shakti. How could an embittered heterophobic femprude understand such a thing?

The feminist movement has always had a problem with prostitution. Not all feminists were against it of course, but abolitionists wanted to wipe it out because they saw it as male control of women's sexuality, which they wanted to end. Much as religion saw prostitutes as the worst instantiation of fornication or sex outside love and marriage, so feminists saw them as the perfect example of slaves to men, serving their sexual needs, disempowered and forced through destitution to become paid objects. Prostitutes perpetuate the ultimate insult, it is argued, not just on themselves but on all women. Prostitution, it is said, is men's crime against women.

When prostitution works as it should do, men and women negotiate on a relatively egalitarian basis and agree on a mutually beneficial contract. I don't believe that prostitution is a symptom of patriarchal oppression of women and therefore that ridding the world of patriarchal values could leave prostitution intact and thriving. As far as generalisations are valid, I believe most heterosexual men have more image-driven libidos than women and are hard-wired to be turned on by feminine bodies. There are those who refute this kind of biological determinism, but for me it is self-evident that men are designed by nature to be able to enjoy sex with women simply because they are physically beautiful. Men need to get erections in order to perform intercourse and they arguably can't get them from the beauty of a woman's mind. Sex is often a separate experience for men from romantic love and if they understand Tantra, sex is transformed from a recreational activity to a deep aesthetic and spiritual experience.

But am I right to draw such a fault line between the sexual profiles of men and women? Maybe some women are more like men than we think, and vice versa. I suspect that women are becoming more willing to confess in public their interest in men's bodies, but until we get past this mess of confused ideas which are actually coming from a residual cesspool of religious prejudice and anti-eroticism, we will be delaying the process by which women can find out what they really want. If femprudes keep stigmatising women in the sex trade and the porn business who number millions, women on the outside will not be able to make free decisions for fear of being damned. If femprudes keep damning men for sexually objectifying women, when will women ever be allowed to sexually objectify men? Personally I believe that intergenerational sex should work as well for women as it does for men and that it should be socially acceptable for older women to buy sex from younger escorts and enjoy physical recreational and Tantric sex with strangers.

I totally reject the popular myth espoused by femprudes that social inequality and injustice are preconditions for prostitution. I don't believe the argument that if poverty, unemployment and low wages were eliminated, prostitution would disappear. This is as near sighted as Karl Marx's risible prediction that religion is the opiate of the people and would disappear if everyone's material needs were met. Both these assumptions are based on a completely false analysis of human nature and the psychosomatic depths of sex and spirituality in the human soul. If prostitution was de-stigmatised and trafficking eliminated and if sex workers were respected as skilled entertainers in the hospitality business or as healers of male loneliness and aesthetic deprivation, I think many women would find sex work not only an attractive option but an altruistic vocation. It is human nature to want to maximise one's standard of living - nobody ever has enough money. Many women with good day jobs in the West choose to make extra cash as escorts in the evening. Prostitution will never be allowed to work properly in a world where the insidious anti-erotic fables of Christianity and Islam have not been totally debunked and dismissed by the state.

None of us operate in a perfect market. I have sexual needs and sex workers have financial needs, and we would both like to make our contract in a better world, but we both have to work with the economic and cultural conditions that prevail, which are beyond our control. I have a financial struggle to get the money to pay for girls. We are both victims of greedy capitalism. I'm not a rich Westerner exploiting a foreign market for cheap sex, but if I was rich it wouldn't stop me - I'd just give them generous tips. The fact that politicians fail to provide full employment or eradicate poverty is not my problem as a sex pilgrim. I will use whatever economic conditions that prevail in a country to my best advantage in order to fulfil my Tantric needs and I have no conscience about this. I am not going to deprive myself of beautiful experiences with beautiful women in the Philippines because they are disadvantaged in a country debilitated with political corruption and incompetence at the highest level. There will never be a world of social justice for all in my lifetime, so I see no need to wait for one before I decide to pay for sex.

Abolitionists say prostitution can't be classed as work because it is unique in 'violating the intimate relationship between self and body', because it splits the self from the body which is lost to the self when it is 'sold'. They go on to say the personal parts of the body should only be shared in love and the vagina should not be used for anything else but love and procreation. But this argument is pure sophistry. The sex worker's body is never sold – she is not a slave in a slave market who gives up all control of her body to others to do with as they wish. She sells a sexual service, not her body.

Let me use an analogy. A tourist wants to get to an offshore island and he asks a woman who owns a boat to take him across. In this analogy her boat is like her body and she offers to take him across for a fee. At all times she is the owner and in control of her boat, but she is offering a service. The prohibitionist accusation that paying for sex reduces women to sexual objects is turned on its head by sex worker activists who say themselves that it is not the client that reduces them to a sexual object but femprudes with their ideological fictions. By their characterisation of the sex worker they sexually objectify her. The belief behind this expression is that since a woman has nothing of value to offer except her sexuality, if she sells it she has sold herself and there is nothing left. Violence in prostitution is partly caused by the attitudes of the patronising abolitionists that label prostitutes as demeaned pathetic victims instead of sex shamans: they themselves are so negative about sex workers they teach men whore-stigma and contempt for sex workers.

The self is never entirely divorced from the body in sex work. It is true that the body is foregrounded in the relationship between sex worker and a customer, but when prostitution is allowed to function as it should there can be a cordial and civilised communication between parties. I often discuss religion with escorts and we exchange views on many subjects. In Asia 'longtime' is more affordable and the communication may take all night. Great care is taken to choose a girl with a good heart and a friendly disposition. Sometimes a customer will take a girl to dinner, or away to a holiday location and sometimes girls even end up in marriage. Alternatively, sometimes they get raped or even murdered and I am not trying to gloss over the dangers these girls face, but I also know of bar girls who scam customers and have multiple foreign boyfriends, all unaware of each other sending money for the same apartment.

Some bar girls do really well out of prostitution and make more than they could ever make in normal employment. A case in point is Hong Kong, where Asian bar girls can make more in one hour than their counterparts working as domestics can make in a month of servitude. I would argue that foreign workers in domestic service in Hong Kong, mainly to Chinese employers, are far more likely to be exploited than their counterparts in the nightclubs.

The contention that the vagina is private and should only be used for love and procreation advanced by some feminists is simply a tiresome rehash of historic religious teachings, and is subjective and opinionated. It is up to women as individuals to use their sexual organs in any way they wish. The privacy argument is no less sophistic and is a hypocritical attempt at false respect for the female sexual organs. This argument by femprudes confuses enforced genital privacy with respect, and is in fact just inverted prudery. Feminist killjoys who criticise beauty contests and sexy pop videos and want women's bodies covered up are slow to recognise that women are the guardians of their own bodies and have the right to use intelligent discretion to de-privatise their bodies for a good reason. Why hide your light under a bushel? Why cover up something beautiful? Men like me who *really* think the vagina is sacred want to paint pictures and write songs and poetry in homage to its beauty. Civilizations that really think the human sex organs are sacred turn them into artistic or religious icons and put them on public view in temples - they don't hide them away in shame under a mound of pseudo-intellectual, academic jargon claiming to be about respect.

The critics argue that women have always had their needs subordinated to those of men, especially men whose sexual needs are hardly of consequence to them outside the marriage bed. They wish to place men's selfish needs in a historical context that demonstrates the appalling catalogue of crimes against women through the ages. I agree with this historical narrative that catalogues the appalling treatment of women by men through the ages, and would add that most of it has been aggravated and exacerbated by patriarchal religion. I think I'm entitled to be defensive here because why should I pay the price for the crimes of my ancestors? I am an existentialist individual – I am not patriarchy personified, and the sins of the fathers cannot be visited on their sons. I have done none of these things to women. But my needs matter. My needs matter, as do the justified needs of all men and women in a world that cares about each other's legitimate right to the pursuit of happiness.

This jaundiced brand of feminism is misandrist and almost theological, because it typecasts most men as exploiters, branded like cattle with original sin. It is also itself sexist and misogynistic, because it is premised on the belief that women are heartless and don't care or shouldn't care about good men's needs just because of the misdeeds of bad men.

It is surely time for men to reassert their right in the post-feminist age to enjoy the beauty of naked women, just as it is their right to enjoy the beauty of any other part of nature. Why is it considered admirable for a man to appreciate the beauty of a full moon but tacky and voyeuristic to contemplate the curves of a woman's naked buttocks in a striptease? Men must start to engage with the spiritual side of non-conjugal sex, which is as much about psychosomatic self-empowerment and the satisfaction of the aesthetic sense as it is about the fulfilment of the libido. What I like about temple prostitution is that it endows the woman with a holiness as a giver of prasada or mana. Ideally I would like all men to see erotic dancers as avatars of the goddess, which of course is asking far too much of the average man in our spiritually decadent times.

As well as the academic arguments against the sex trade there are more visceral objections that people just feel whether you like it or not. The sight, or even the thought, of a man in his sixties or seventies having sex with an 18-year-old reminds people of incest or even paedophilia and looks 'wrong'. What possible rapport, objectors ask, can men and women have across such an age gap? But I believe that just because intergenerational sex may look like incest, it is definitely not incest, and therefore this cannot be a serious moral objection. I believe that Tantra actually favours or prioritises older people's needs over the young. Young men and women, unless they have special problems, should not have to use sex workers. They should play the field with a view to marriage and procreation, but once their children have spread their wings and left the nest, men and women are faced with a new future in which they are free to recreate themselves. If they are so inclined to embrace Tantra their sex life can experience a sea change and a multi-dimensional transformation where interpersonal sex and human intimacy is replaced with supra-personal sex and a new intimacy with the universe through sex. This holds true for the divorced or singles or for married couples who might still love each other but are bored with each other sexually.

I agree that aesthetically speaking, the sight of old people engaged in sex with much younger people is not pretty, but this is merely a matter of aesthetics. The ugliness of senescence coupling with youth is no cause for censorship. Prostitution is for me primarily about the elderly using the bodies of youth as a spiritual rocket fuel, and communication across the generation gap is quite adequate for this purpose and would improve if sex workers had more understanding of Tantra and the needs of elderly sex pilgrims. Sometimes it's a pleasant relief to have a simple uncomplicated communication which may be not much more than small talk because of the language barrier, but at least it is upfront and honest because both know the agreed outcome. There are no mind games with a sex worker and therefore conversation is refreshingly candid and is not used as a disingenuous cover for seduction.

New legislation is growing in popularity throughout Europe to criminalise citizens who pay for sex. They argue that paying for sex demeans both men and women and provides the matrix for trafficking of prostitutes, sexual slavery and child prostitution. I think this an egregious distortion of the facts. Prostitution, child abuse and woman trafficking are often unfairly conflated by politicians, but they are in fact separate issues. Of course in the real world they overlap, but trafficking is wrong because it is forced prostitution, while voluntary prostitution is a social good and trafficking should not be used as an excuse to get rid of decent sex work. It is a complete cop-out by politicians to blame men and women like me for their miserable failure to eradicate the social evils that feed off legitimate prostitution.

Not all feminists are against prostitution, of course.

Nickie Roberts, an ex-prostitute, wrote a very informative history of whores. She argued that whores were the first feminists and the first to say no to patriarchal ownership. In times of goddess worship, shamanic priestesses channelled the creative energy of the goddess into the material world. They were ecstatic women using trance and dance. It was during the transition from matriarchy to patriarchy that the sacred sexual power of women became socialised into the first instances of sacred temple prostitution. Many of the Babylonian priestesses were singers and dancers and performed sexual rites – the earnings of prostitutes were made in the name of the goddess and meant as offerings to Ishtar.

I recognise that sacred prostitution was always contaminated by patriarchal exploitation of women, but through all this contamination in every age the shamanistic fusion of woman as sex donor, shaman and dancer shines through like an abiding pulsar of hope and peacemaking in the male killing fields all around them.

Judaic monotheists were some of the first patriarchal fanatics and expositors of whore abolition. Centuries before Christ they invaded goddess-worshipping Canaan and tried to stamp out the whore priestesses. Prostitution will never be understood in our own times if we don't view it in its historical context vis à vis its troubled relationship through the ages with monotheism, which subconsciously, and sometimes consciously, sees the dancer-whore as the devil's succubus and a dangerous atavistic reminder of the mother goddess and pagan sexual liberty.

This is an intended insult every sex worker should embrace as a compliment of the highest order. As the devil's succubus she is also the unwitting muse of the Antichrist, whether she knows it or not. In the eyes of monotheism the whore is the lowest and most brazen of all fornicators, a woman who reduces love to a cheap commodity to sell for a pittance in a contract of mutual abuse. It is important in the battles that lie ahead that the whore knows her enemy, and if she wears a crucifix she should remove it and be true to herself and to the God that does not threaten her with eternal physical torments in the next world. Just as it is the height of hypocrisy for gay people to remain Muslims or Christians, so it is two-faced for sex workers to belong to religions that expect them to feel shame for showing sexual generosity to their needy fellow human beings.

CHAPTER FIVE

Conceptual Art
As Revolution

My aim in this chapter is to bring to light certain aspects
of the philosophy of art that are relevant to my own work,
and in doing this to give some anecdotal substance to my
own opinions about what constitutes good art. I am
particularly interested in the concept of symbolism in art
and symbolism that relates to political and religious ideas.
For example, Christian art through the centuries has the
primary function of illustrating, celebrating and explaining
Biblical narratives and is also morally prescriptive and
didactic. I strongly disagree with the Christian message,
but I totally embrace the idea of art offering solutions to
world problems and moral guidance and support the

concept of an official state-sponsored art as long as the state embodies enlightened ideas.

My paintings do not just rely on visual symbolism because they include text that is integrated into the erotic imagery as an aesthetic formal element, so the political and metaphysical message of my art work is clear. Modern art has also given rise to some dynamic ideological art which has attempted to embody political and metaphysical ideas that I want to briefly mention and relate to my own work. These include the Futurists and De Stijl. Finally I want to mention the artists I most admire and why, and perhaps this is my way of saying what I think is good art.

Iconology is the study of icons and their symbolic meanings. Without wishing to put a finer point on definitions, heraldic blazons, insignia, flags, and road signs are all symbols, otherwise known as ideograms or pictograms. Freemasonry, alchemy and astrology also have their own repertoire of signs. A pictogram or ideogram is a visual symbol – often abstract - that represents ideas and concepts. The death's head or the skull and cross bones is an example of a well-known pictogram symbolising the fearsome pirate ship. The national flag is an amazing ideogram that symbolises a whole raft of ideas representing a nation, its identity and its aspirations. The national flag of India is supercharged with highly complex pictographic symbolism, which is hardly surprising given the complex polytheistic nature of Hinduism. Sometimes, as in the case of the swastika for example, an emblem is adopted or adapted by many different cultures and religions, with different symbolism being attributed to it through the ages.

I have already made reference to the prehistoric vulvic

pictogram in which the schematic vulva symbolised divine cosmic creation and women's birthing powers. Even the human body, especially in Indian dance, can be used as a form of sign language via the use of *mudra*s or hand gestures. The female body has itself been adopted by political groups and countries throughout history, perhaps the most famous being woman personified as Reason in the French revolution. But what enabled her to personify Reason? It was simply the arbitrary will of others to give her this title with its symbolic associations. In the same way, I have the right to arbitrarily invest any of my images with any symbolism I wish, and it is up to the viewer to learn these symbols if he or she wishes to understand my work at its deepest levels. If the effort of investigating my philosophy is too much, then my work can still be enjoyed at a purely aesthetic level.

The French cult of reason was a revolutionary anti-clerical protest against Christianity. Many churches were turned into temples and in Notre Dame, renamed the Temple of Reason, a beautiful woman was chosen to ritually represent Reason, Truth and Liberty in what was called the Feast of Reason. Where the high altar had stood there was now a temple of philosophy. I hope the reader will accept this as a precedent for my own artwork, which portrays the feminine form as *imago dei*, or God's greatest aesthetic masterpiece, and Asian go-go dancers as living ideograms of peace and love in the world with a rich heritage stretching back to sacred temple prostitution.

Christian iconography is rich in symbolism. The complex semiotic richness of a simple and seemingly straightforward image can perhaps best be explained with a reference to Agnus Dei – the Lamb of God. On one level it is just a depiction of a lamb balancing a cross on one of its front hooves. For those who recall that St John the Baptist said "Behold the Lamb of God that takes away the sins of the world", the image can be seen as another way of depicting Jesus. Then for those who have read the Old Testament, the Jewish idea of the lamb as a sacrificial animal will be added to the picture. The ideas of gentleness and purity, of innocence, whiteness, simplicity and freshness, all the attributes that have been associated with lambs, will attach themselves to the image, bringing us to the loaded concept of the totally sinless sacrificial victim offered as an expiation of another's guilt. The originally simple image has become a substitute for a depiction of Jesus, an innocent creature, a destined victim or a bearer of others' sins. Yet it is also a sign to believers of the triumph of the Cross and therefore of Resurrection. In this view a symbol may be likened to a stone thrown into a lake with the rings of associated ideas extending outward.

Of course the most obvious and iconic symbol of Christianity is the cross. During the Iconoclast rule, which lasted with intermissions from 725 to 824, naturalistic representations of Christ were forbidden by the Orthodox authorities in Constantinople. A cross is an abstract symbol and this was allowed by the image haters - the Iconoclasts - but a figurative image of Christ was forbidden. But what is important here is that if the state has a worldview that it wants its citizens to embrace and understand, then it makes sense to have an iconography that explains and reinforces the state ideology. If the state is wrong-minded and its propaganda delusional, then the art will reflect this and it won't seem such a good idea.

Nazi art would be the first example that springs to mind, but Christianity also is arguably delusional, and the Sistine Chapel in the Vatican proudly displays the obscene painting by Michelangelo of the Last Judgement which depicts sinners with lurid sadistic relish being tortured in the afterlife for all eternity. Art debases itself if it dignifies hell, because whereas other superstitions that are celebrated in art can be excused away by pre-scientific ignorance, the evil of hell is self-evident through *a priori* logic and reason, which are theoretically constant in every age and culture from the dawn of history. Surely the ancient Hindu and Greek philosophers prove that ancient peoples are just as capable of logical thinking as we are. There's no excuse in any age for the *non sequitur* of a good and merciful God torturing his creatures for ever. At the end of the day, good art has to illustrate the truth not falsehoods. This is surely why we don't like Nazi art, even though it is aesthetically acceptable. We don't treasure it because it celebrates lies and untruths.

If we now turn to modern art, we enter a passionate debate about many fascinating arguments and issues. When I was at art school it was often said that if an artist has to explain his work, or talk about his work to get it across, he has already failed. The visual arts are supposed to be about seeing and feeling and the challenge for a painter or sculptor is to say the whole thing without resorting to words. Some argue that artists should not be theoreticians, and even Cézanne said to an artist friend "Do not be an art critic, but paint, therein lies salvation."

Picasso also held this point of view, and said that trying to understand art was as futile as trying to understand the song of a bird and that if he painted a hammer and sickle it was not meant to symbolise communism because he only wanted to "reproduce the objects for what they are and not for what they mean." But even Picasso admitted his monumental work *Guernica* expressed a deliberate sense of propaganda.

The Futurist movement was the brainchild of poet Filippo Marinetti, who attracted a group of painters who were influenced by his ideas and had their first exhibition in 1911. Here was the most blatant fusion of political ideology and art. The Futurists actually produced their own political manifesto which stated their beliefs and aims: "We intend to glorify the love of danger... the beauty of speed... We will glorify war – the only true hygiene."

They showed contempt for women and feminism and recommended the destruction of museums and libraries. Their ideas were arguably infantile and destined to be ephemeral, but the important issue for me is that here, art and politics came together, creating a new dynamic and a utopian prescriptive recipe for the future. The anarchistic radicalism of Futurism was highly refreshing, if naive. They denounced art critics and most artists before them and glorified the madman who rejected moralism and convention, and worst of all from my point of view, they went out of their way to rant against the nude as a motif in art which they denounced as "nauseous and tedious" and stated "To paint from the posing model is an absurdity, and an act of mental cowardice, even if the model be translated upon the picture in linear, spherical or cubic forms."

The purest of the abstract movements was the Dutch group De Stijl, founded in 1917; one of its major artists was Piet Mondrian. De Stijl was a model for the perfect harmony, and believed it possible both for man as an individual and society as a whole. It thus had an ethical and even a spiritual mission. Mondrian regarded his art as a philosophical and religious expression. He hoped in some way society would adopt his principles of artistic harmony so that the world would become one huge abstract masterpiece. If the world itself was an artistic masterpiece, he said, there would be no need for paintings because we would live in "the midst of realized art."

Mondrian was a very spiritual abstract artist and was focused on understanding universal beauty and universal truth through his art, which he believed it could improve society: "A great scholar has recently said that pure science achieves practical results for humanity. Similarly, one can say that pure art, even though it appears abstract, can be of direct utility for life."

Perhaps the diametrical opposite of symbolism is abstract art, which was pioneered by visionaries like Malevich. This is important to me because my own artwork is semi-abstract and my images of the vulva are schematic and stylised because I don't like illusionist or imitative art. Kasamir Malevich was one of the great founders of abstract art and his philosophy emphasised the importance of feeling and subjectivity. In his style, known as Suprematism, pure feeling undiluted with thoughts is what he wanted to engender in the viewer. To the Suprematist the visual phenomena of the objective world are, in themselves, meaningless; the significant thing is feeling, as such, quite apart from the environment in which it is called forth.

The square, never to be found in nature, was the basic element in Suprematism. It was not an empty square, Malevich insisted. It was full of the absence of any object, and it was pregnant with meaning. He never subscribed to the belief that art should serve a utilitarian purpose. Love of the square and abstract purity attracted public criticism which accused him of destroying art, but he insisted his geometric forms were the future of art. Hence the imitation of nature and the art of representing objects – objectivism was irrelevant to Malevich, who embraced non-objective abstract Suprematism, which reaches a 'desert' in which "nothing can be perceived but feeling".

Like Mondrian and other deep thinking artists, he arguably made overblown claims for his work. To cross that historic faultline between representational art and abstract art is undoubtedly one of the great achievements of humankind in the field of the visual arts, but whether simple squares can really produce the emotional intensity in viewers that he wished for is a moot point. His art is arguably the total opposite of the Futurists, because its *raison d'être* is the elimination of ideas - an art that in his own words has "divested itself of the ballast of religious and political ideas". His belief that objective figurative art was now obsolete and pointless also turned out to be untrue.

Dada was a movement of negation but political nonetheless. In contrast to Futurists, Dadaists professed a disgust for war, and one of its leading exponents was

Marcel Duchamp, who was also a conceptual artist. In its manifesto it declared its commitment to communism, demanding the requisition of churches and the submission of all laws and decrees to the Dadaist central council for approval. But perhaps the most nutty of all its ideas is the immediate regulation of all sexual behaviour according to the views of international Dadaism through the establishment of a Dadaist sexual centre!

Dada denounced the art world as being a merely commercial enterprise in which artists were hostage to its bourgeois capitalist decadence. Marcel Duchamp epitomised the anti-establishment stance of both Dada and conceptualism when in 1917 he entered a urinal, his infamous 'Readymade' for an exhibition. This is generally seen as the quintessential 'proto-conceptual' artefact, establishing the principle that art related more to the artist's intentions than to anything he did with his hands or felt about beauty: art as idea. Dada mocked mankind's pride in its own rationalism and celebrated the senseless, and trumpeted the praises of unreason – or as one follower put it, "Dada gave the Venus de Milo an enema" and set out to destroy notions of good taste.

At the end of the nineteenth century many artists and writers desired a reintegration in which art was to serve a "Utopian brotherhood of man":

The Expressionists too dreamed of a renewal of society in which art could take the place once occupied by religion. The Bauhaus set out to train artists and craftsmen to participate in an expanding industrial society." (Theories of Modern Art, Herschel B. Chipp, P 456)

True art, which is not content to play variations on ready-made models but rather insists on expressing the inner needs of man and of mankind in its time – true art is unable not to be revolutionary, not to aspire to a complete and radical reconstruction of society. (Theories of Modern Art, P. 484)

Andre Breton and Leon Trotsky proclaimed their belief in "complete freedom for art" in their Manifesto and defined the role of the true artist in a decadent society as a political revolutionary:

The Communist revolution is not afraid of art. It realizes that the role of the artist in a decadent capitalist society is determined by the conflict between the individual and various social forms that are hostile to him. This fact alone, insofar as he is conscious of it, makes the artist the natural ally of revolution... No, painting is not done to decorate apartments. It is an instrument of war for attack and defence against the enemy. (Theories of Modern Art, P. 484)

The history of modern art can sometimes be seen as a series of 'isms', many hardly distinguishable from each other, but some of them are landmarks in the evolution of human aesthetics. Primitivism, personified by artists like Modigliani, was about Western artists being influenced by earlier cultures, and their art styles including Japanese art, Egyptian and African art and Bronze age Cycladic. Constructivism, embodied by Vladimir Tatlin, collapsed the distinction between sculpture and architecture and proposed that art should have a direction and social application. Fauvism was the name of a group of Parisian painters, among them Henri Matisse, who around the turn of the nineteenth century were painting works characterised by wild, vivid unrealistic colours. Trees could be bright pink and grass blue, and all that mattered was that all this fandango of colours produced the right emotional reaction.

The use of unrealistic colour is certainly an important part of my own work. When I paint the vulva I use vivid, unrealistic colours to enhance their likeness to flowers. When I paint the anal starburst I use colours similar to multi-coloured galaxies. The starburst actually resembles ancient spoked pagan sun symbols and should be regarded as just another natural form that is echoed throughout the universe with various homologues. Many of the great modern artists were deeply concerned with spiritual matters. Matisse wrote "What interests me most is neither still life nor landscape but the human figure. It is through it that I best succeed in expressing the nearly religious feeling that I have towards life".

The Bauhaus established in 1919 aimed to unify avant garde visual art with design and architecture for the improvement of society. The aims of the Bauhaus could hardly be more different from those of the existentialists. Existentialism was a philosophy elucidated by Jean-Paul Sartre and painters like Francis Bacon illustrated themes of human angst and the futility of existence without God or meaning. But what is noteworthy is the frequent crossover and sharing between the different disciplines from poetry, politics and philosophy, to painting and sculpture and architecture. Art served as a crucible in which a heady cocktail of human aspirations fused into a creative dynamic that at times had lofty ambitions to change the world.

In contrast to these noble dreams for the betterment of humankind, pop art was a movement that reflected the superficiality of its surrounding popular culture. This art form appropriated the lowbrow images found in mass media sources, from consumer advertisements and comic strips to magazine photo-shoots and movies. Andy Warhol is perhaps the most famous and charismatic exponent of pop art. This genre did not attempt to improve the world with utopian visions but to report it and reflect it as it was with all its gimmicky superficiality.

In contrast to pop art, conceptualism was about important ideas and concepts being more relevant than the formal items themselves and in a sense transcending them and having a life outside the artefact. Spectators who viewed these works were seen more as "receivers" or people who received ideas rather than viewers who viewed pictures that are pleasing to the eye, because aesthetics were not of great importance in conceptual art.

I have only covered a fraction of all the art movements and 'isms', but I hope I have done enough to provide useful examples that will help me better justify my own work. To me, good art has to work on as many fronts as possible. It must be dynamic aesthetically with a good use of colour, which means the colours have potent reactions to each other and must not only sing in tune but sing moving melodies. It needs to be conceptually rich and original. Van Gogh is a great artist in my view, because he is the only artist who has actually captured the life force. In some of his works like *Wheat Field with Cypresses* and

Starry Night the sky explodes with cosmic energy. No artist has ever achieved this Tantric pantheist miracle so successfully and believe it or not Van Gogh was a Christian! Turner may be famous for capturing the superficial passing moods of weather, but Van Gogh captured eternity and the very essence of the universe behind the ephemera. The artist is merely a channel and Van Gogh's genius came from a higher power that transcended his Christian delusions.

Paul Gauguin is another artist whose style is not only beautiful but so original. He worked in Tahiti creating mystical images of a primal sexual paradise of pagan innocence. His paintings to me are Tantric celebrations of life and its central meaning, which is joy and exultation in the privilege of being alive and being able to witness the universe in all its majesty and mystery.

I don't believe in the modern art market, which is money driven and held hostage to unscrupulous collectors and dealers who often buy and sell art simply for its investment value. I believe in a national state art that would express the virtues and insights of Natural Religion and provide regular employment for hundreds or perhaps thousands of state artists and craftsmen. Individual artists would still be free to follow their own calling but the state could provide an aesthetic gold standard and stability where artists and public alike would know what was good and bad art. I believe the entrepreneurial era of the great individual artist has probably passed its heyday and it is now time for painting, sculpture and especially architecture to serve a higher purpose as the visual language of a new world order.

I hope I have demonstrated that art and artists are historically often about expressing philosophical and religious ideas and even about critiquing the world and recommending changes. Or equally art can be about celebrating and illustrating a state religion or political system. I don't think any of the art visions have come to much in this age dominated by anarchy, corruption, poverty, human rights violations and ISIL's unprecedented brutality. Daesh has given us YouTube videos of innocent people being beheaded and burned alive – a perfect reminder of a far worse fate allotted to infidels in the next world! The modern art world today has lost its soul, and to a great extent avoids confronting taboos within the two burning issues of our times, namely sex and religion, which are the areas in which the most humbug, hypocrisy, and mendacity thrive, largely unchallenged. I believe my paintings at least pass my own criteria for good art. They are aesthetically pleasing and original and embody recommendations for radically improving the world.

Above all, I would like the reader to recall the earlier comparison made between a symbol and a stone thrown into a pond that ripples out with multiple meanings. This is how I want my images of the feminine body to be seen and appreciated, namely as revolutionary Tantric ideograms. The schematized vulva serves me and my Tantric art as a pictogram. It not only symbolises my own sexual pleasure, but also the paradox of women as erotic dancers, peacemakers, and sexual vendors side by side with seditious Antichrist feminism as Mary Daly envisioned it. In conceptual art, the intention of the artist is what defines his art and in my own mind the feminine body and its erogenous zones, especially the vulvic motif that I use in almost every painting, is emblematic of the genesis of revolutionary feminism. It is the feminist Antichrist instantiated in militant cunt power and woman-spirit-rising. Kali, the ferocious warrior aspect or avatar of Shakti emerges in my vision from Aphrodite – her opposite – the divine whore and love goddess. From divine whore and stripper to shamanistic Kali warrior, women could come out fighting, finally disgracing the sadosociety with their ultimate weapon of social transformation, namely dance and more specifically, strategic protest dancing or guerrilla dance. 'Make love not war' is the theory and prostitution and guerrilla dance is the praxis. Radical change could come from a seemingly unlikely catalyst if women started a campaign of strategic protest dancing against hellfire superstition outside churches, synagogues and mosques – a campaign that was willing even to go naked at some point if that was what it took to get world peace on track. They would undoubtedly put themselves in harm's way and some might be imprisoned or worse, but their campaign would ignite debate all over the world and would attract so much media attention that they could in time perhaps shock the world into change. Maybe it is too hopeful to expect a mass global movement, but small groups of determined activists feeding their videos into the social media might just be enough to pack a big punch beyond their weight.

The world listens to women these days and sees them as proven changemakers and self-liberators. It is doubtful if women who already occupy hard-won positions of power, wealth and influence can ever change the system from within. They are already conformists and collaborators, trained by patriarchy to mimic men and their metaphysical delusions and trapped in the foothills of the end time with very little wiggle room to 'make love not war'. Maybe it's quixotic and unfeasible, but I wonder what effect it would have if this new grass-roots activism emerged – an Antichrist, Kali-driven movement to overthrow the male sadogods calling itself 'WAH' perhaps - Women Against Hell?

Women will never get equality with men until they reconfigure God: until they prove to men that they have a better alternative to the conceptual abortion at the heart of monotheism. Naming and defining God is the ultimate act of human self-empowerment, and until women realise this they will remain disempowered. Men will always feel superior while they have the kudos of being the god-makers. It is the greatest irony of the post-feminist age that liberated women remain so naive that they believe a man when he comes down from a mountain and announces he knows the mind of God! How can any woman not see through such egotistical megalomania? Anyone who claims he knows what God thinks has no appreciation of infinity and the astronomical complexity of the universe. Any man who claims to know the mind of God knows only his own conceit.

CHAPTER SIX

Make Love Not War – The Eros Mantra

This is the ballad of a hippy girl
They called her 'make love not war'
She kept the company of dreamers
But she knew what love was for
chorus: *make love not war –*
why don't they say it any more?
She was scared of Hiroshima
She saw napalm in Vietnam
The cold war broke her heart
With bombs to blow the world apart
She saw children die like flies

From foolish wars made by lies
And her answer was peace and love
A new religion from God above
There's no hell or heaven
In her new revelation
But the world called her a whore
For making love not war
chorus. *Make love not war –*
why don't they say it any more?

song by the author

'Make love not war' is a slogan from the hippy era which has a retro feel to it now, suggesting idealistic dreamers and lotus eaters, fused perhaps in the public mind with John Lennon and his peace protests. The song above is one of many I've written and performed in public to promote the ideas and ideals expressed in my books and paintings. I believe the Eros mantra needs to be revived big time and given some sleek new contours and some sharp teeth to bite through all the warmongering bullshit that politicians are talking today. 'Make love not war' is pure Tantra and the world needs this mantra more than anything else today. The mantra embraces Eros and spurns Thanatos – the death instinct. Eros is the life force and the love of life. It is pagan 'wonderlust' for the universe. Thanatos is suicide, monotheism and the death cults.

The Eros mantra attests that sex is the life force of the universe because it arguably represents the thirst of the universe for self-awareness through procreation. It represents the pleasure principle and the human need for ecstasy and happiness. The pursuit of happiness is our common human goal, but human selfishness and human stupidity in so many ways prevent this common goal from being realised. We need new leaders who are capable of lateral thinking and work hard to eliminate, not just the obvious causes of division and separatism like racism and selfish capitalism, but the less obvious ones like hellfire superstition and nationalism. It is difficult to see how such new visionary leaders can emerge unless there is a massive sea change and paradigm shift in grass roots public opinion.

The Eros Mantra tells us that we need spiritually-enlightened politicians dedicated to the ideal of the world citizen, a world federation and ultimately a world government. We need politicians who believe passionately in eventually phasing out nationalism and sectarian tribal mindsets and who will work to establish a new co-humanity, a new human fellowship based on rational spiritual values. This new global mono-religion will replace doctrinal religion and bigoted holy books with a broad inclusive spirituality that allows individual interpretations of God but with two provisos.

Firstly no one has the right to believe in a God of eternal torture unless they can produce empirical evidence for the existence of hell, and secondly, everyone should try and understand that however they interpret the God-word, their interpretations are only symbols of the Unknown God – the Absolute that is ineffable and beyond our present understanding. For me, God is sex, namely the yab-yum, but this is just mythopoetic storytime. I don't believe this is anything else but a metaphor for the unknown. Everybody is entitled to have their own storytime which helps them relate to the ineffable Absolute. The only thing we know for sure about this God - the real God – is that it is immeasurably powerful – not necessarily omnipotent but at least as powerful as Nature because it is by definition, the power source and sustainer of the cosmos.

I don't believe in knocking monotheism unless you can replace it with something better. Transhumanism today, to most people, means the philosophy that believes in humankind remaking itself and even one day replacing itself through the utilisation of advanced technologies. These include technologies that are already well established and more futuristic technologies that are anticipated like molecular nanotechnology and artificial intelligence. I'm a believer in this understanding of transhumanism, but it is vital that modern transhumanists reconnect the modern movement with its original founder and purpose, namely Julian Huxley, who emphasised the importance of a non-monotheist spirituality. The present transhumanist movement is not truly transhumanist and will fill the world with more insoluble problems unless it has a correct metaphysical compass.

Julian Huxley believed in Natural Religion which is entirely rooted in the information science gives us about the universe. His worldview was not perfect, but he didn't claim to be an infallible prophet transmitting a revelation from God, just a simple man using his unaided reason in an infinitely complex and mysterious cosmos. The word 'transhumanism' itself was coined by Julian Huxley, who wrote a ground-breaking book entitled 'Religion without

Revelation' which was published in the nineteen-sixties. Transhumanism is a form of humanism that transcends secularism and engages the numinous. Huxley had the unique insight to realise that humanism and secularism are not enough if humanity needs to move beyond its superstitions; humanism needs to recognise the god-shaped hole in the human heart and offer humanity spiritual options that are compatible with science and reason. Hence transhumanism is humanism that transcends itself by recognising the importance of 'religion', but Natural Religion, not supernatural religion.

This religion would have only one holy book, namely the book of Nature, revealed to us through philosophy, art and science. Natural religion does not recognise revelatory knowledge because such pseudo-knowledge is based on blind faith instead of reason and empirical evidence. This is a "unitary vision" he wrote where "all kinds of splits and dualisms and healed". The divine, he correctly argues, is not supernatural but "what man finds worthy of adoration, that which compels his awe."

The religion of the future is about releasing the massive untapped human potential that could make a new and better world. "A humanist religion will have to work out its own rituals and its own basic symbolism." The great task of science will be "to create a religion for humanity." What is, he asks, the essence of Godliness or spirituality? It is 'awe', 'mystery', 'wonder', 'reverence', he argues, and with this I am in total agreement. 'God' is just a word I use to describe the humbling human experience, the unique emotion of boundless awe when we are confronted with the mysterious universe. He argued that religion does not need a Supreme Being. Religion is about reverence and reason. It is true that religion does not need a Supreme Being, but transhumanism is not atheism and it leaves room for such an entity if believers want to articulate their numinous awe experience in that way.

Religion should be rooted in science, not revelation he says. Creeds are dangerous because they become idols and immune to criticism and clog the wheels of progress; they are static and not evolutionary. The quest for truth and God has to be progressive, and religion is static not progressive. Those interested in this debate about a new religion often disagree about whether to keep the God-word or not. Huxley wanted to drop it because it had too much baggage. The God-word is so associated with a supernatural being that we should reject it, and he suggests the term 'Sacred Reality' as an alternative. All religion is man-made, he argued, which is why religiously-minded people and scientifically-minded people must come together to build a common ideology.

Transhumanism is unifying and synergistic from top to bottom, thereby healing all rifts and dualisms. Cosmologically speaking, it is monistic, meaning that matter and energy are different states of the same world stuff. Art and the celebration of truth and beauty are vital. We need to evolve an integrated world society with a commonality of ideals. It will have to develop its own rituals and buildings. For me this means that transhumanism will need its own Tantric temples and its own pantheon of symbolic deities. I will let Huxley speak for himself with the following quotes from his highly under-acclaimed masterpiece of metaphysical pragmatism:

What the sciences discover about the natural world and about the origin, nature, and destiny of man is the truth for religion. There is no other kind of valid knowledge. This natural knowledge, organized and applied to human fulfilment, is the basis of the new and permanent natural religion. (preface)

…"religion must now ally itself wholeheartedly with science… For without the fullest aid from science, we will assuredly not be able to bring into being a religion adequate to our needs" (PP 160 -161)

In this unitary vision, all kinds of splits and dualisms are healed. The entire cosmos is made out of one and the same world-stuff operated by the same energy as we are ourselves. "Mind" and "matter" appear as two aspects of our unitary mind bodies. There is no separate supernatural realm: all phenomena are part of one natural process of evolution. There is no basic cleavage between science and religion; they are both organs of evolving humanity. (P.1)

Today we must melt down the gods and refashion the material into new and effective organs of religion, enabling a man to exist freely and fully on the spiritual level as well as on the material. (P.5)

Meanwhile, religious rituals and moral codes will have to be readapted or remodelled. Besides what Nietzsche called the transvaluation of values, we shall need a transfiguration of thought, a new religious terminology and a reformulation of religious ideas and concepts in a new idiom. A humanist religion will have to work out its own rituals and its own basic symbolism. (P.6)

We need a name for this new belief. Perhaps "transhumanism" will serve: man remaining man, but transcending himself, by realizing new possibilities of and for his human nature. (P 195)

Another great believer in the world citizen and the new world order was Nobel Prize winner Bertrand Russell, who died in 1970, a distinguished British philosopher in logic and the theory of logic. He was also a political visionary and one of the great heretics in morals and religion. As an academic he was persecuted in America for his anti-Christian views and his liberal ideas on sex and nudity. In one of his insightful books, entitled *Why I am not a Christian,* he outlined his many objections to Christianity and religion in general:

"I think all the great religions of the world – Buddhism, Hinduism, Christianity, Islam, and Communism - both untrue and harmful." (preface)

He raises an important objection I wholeheartedly agree with, that Jesus himself, according to biblical texts, expected to return in the second coming within a few decades of his death. Where then is this Judgement day two thousand years after his demise? Why are not Christians acutely embarrassed by his non-arrival, I wonder? But then Russell delivers his punchline, which in my view immediately elevates him to a new human status as a "knower" - someone who knows the truth about Jesus and his dark side:

There is one very serious defect to my mind in Christ's moral character, and that is that He believed in hell. I do not myself feel that any person who is really profoundly humane can believe in everlasting punishment. Christ certainly as depicted in the Gospels did believe in everlasting punishment... (P22)

Then Christ says: "The Son of Man shall send forth His angels, and they shall gather out of His kingdom all things that offend, and them which do iniquity, and shall cast them into a furnace of fire; there shall be wailing and gnashing of teeth"; and He goes on about the wailing and gnashing of teeth. It comes in one verse after another, and it is quite manifest to the reader that there is a certain pleasure in contemplating wailing and gnashing of teeth, or else it would not occur so often. Then you all, of course, remember about the sheep and the goats; how at the second coming to divide the sheep and the goats He is going to say to the goats:" Depart from me, ye cursed into everlasting fire." ...I must say that I think all this doctrine, that hellfire is a punishment for sin, is a doctrine of cruelty. It is a doctrine that put cruelty into the world and generations of cruel torture; and the Christ of the Gospels, if you could take Him as His chroniclers represent Him, would certainly have to be considered partly responsible for that. (P.23)

I say quite deliberately that the Christian religion, as organised in its Churches, has been the principal enemy of moral progress in the world. (P25)

He makes the valid point that religion is not just untrue and anti-rational but it is the major obstacle to world peace and human progress:

The knowledge exists by which universal happiness can be secured; the chief obstacle to its utilisation for that purpose is the teaching of religion. Religion prevents our children from having a rational education; religion prevents us from removing the fundamental causes of war; religion prevents us from teaching the ethic of scientific co-operation in place of the old fierce doctrines of sin and punishment. It is possible that mankind is on the threshold of a golden age; but, if so, it will be necessary first to slay the dragon that guards the door, and this dragon is religion. (P. 42)

Neither Nature or God can give us moral values. We decide ourselves arbitrarily through rational debate what is good and evil and what is right or wrong. Man is the measure. This is often known as 'situational ethics' and it must replace the fictional morality from the ogre in the sky.

In the world of values, Nature in itself is neutral, neither good nor bad, deserving of neither admiration nor censure. It is we who create value and our desires which confer value. In this realm we are kings, and we debase our kingship if we bow down to Nature. It is for us to determine the good life, not for Nature – not even for Nature personified as God. (P. 48)

Russell also wrote *New Hopes for a Changing World*, which tries to breathe new life into a concept politicians seem to have forgotten about, namely the world citizen:

Nationalism is in our day the chief obstacle to the extension of social cohesion beyond national boundaries. It is therefore the chief force making for the extermination of the human race. (P.68)

He believed in a world government:

There is only one way in which the world can be made safe from war, and that is the creation of a single world-wide authority, possessing a monopoly of all the more serious weapons. (p.97)

But it is naive to think this world government can be established peacefully by consent he argues – it will have to be fought for perhaps as a last resort through war:

I do not believe that the human race has sufficient statesmanship or capacity for mutual forbearance to establish a world Government on a basis of consent alone. That is why I think that an element of force will be needed in its establishment and in its preservation through the early years of its existence. (P. 98)

Racism is divisive and racial purity is an obstacle to world peace, therefore there should be more interracial marriage. The races should mix together, he says, and I totally agree with ending ethnic and racial separatism especially in the case of the Jews, whose costly obsession with their own exceptionalism is seen by some as racist. The whole idea of a chosen people of God in the twenty-first century is repugnant to reason and an affront to world citizenship. The Judaists should renounce their absurd claim to be God's favourites and end thousands of years of self-righteous religious separatism by choosing assimilation instead:

Where racially distinct populations have to live side by side, the only solution is complete intermixture. This is objected to usually on one side and sometimes on both. Orthodox Jews have a horror of marrying Gentiles, much stronger than any Gentile prejudice against marrying Jews (except among the Nazis). This is regrettable. It would be much better if the separateness of Jews came to an end, and people ceased to notice whether a person was a Jew or not. (P.113)

In terms of my own worldview, Transhumanism must include elements of Tantric ideology. The following quotes are from Alain Danielou's book *Shiva and the Primordial Tradition*. He was a renowned Western expert on Tantra, and he was concerned to point out that Shaivite philosophy - that is Tantra based in the worship of Shiva and the phallus - knows no dogma and he is fundamentally opposed to monotheism because 'God' or the world principle is ineffable and should remain a mystery.

Monotheism is therefore a metaphysical error, since the world principle, which is outside the world, is beyond number, impersonal, indescribable, and unknowable. Above all, monotheism is dangerous because of its consequences, since it is a projection of the human "self" into the divine sphere, replacing love and respect for the divine work as a whole with a fictitious character, a kind of heavenly king who governs human affairs, to whom the most absurd edicts are attributed. Intolerant, the so-called "only god" is, in fact, only the god of one tribe. Monotheistic religions have served as an excuse for persecutions, massacres, and genocides; they fight each other to impose the dominion of their heavenly tyrant on others. (P4)

He recognised that if the sexual organs are celebrated in Tantra so also must be their procreative powers:

The rites of procreation are carefully described in the Tantras. They include worship of the organs, the images of the divine principles that will unite to accomplish the miracle. Not seeing the image of the divine principle in the procreative organs and not worshipping them as such is the first step toward moral decay and the degradation of the species. (P.31)

Tantra puts the human body and human sexuality slap bang in the middle of transhumanism. Christianity and Islam are arguably anti-erotic death cults, but Tantra is hedonistic, pro-life and pro-pleasure. Tantra glorifies the human body because its justified. The Tantric concept of the human form is the *totalised body* - the human body as the greatest phenomenon in the known universe.

Again I can best explain this concept on a personal anecdotal level. When I look at a sexy go-go dancer the first thing I think of, I confess, is sex. I want to take her back to the hotel and document her beauty photographically, then make love to her. But at a deeper level I know I am making love to a generic miracle: the miracle of the human body that can dance in a thousand different styles and excel in a thousand different sports, can play a thousand different musical instruments and so on.

Not only is the human body capable of all these disparate skills but it is a biological mind-fuck. If you think what is actually going on in a dancer's body as she moves at a molecular and cellular level the mind boggles. As if this isn't enough, the body that gyrates, bumps and grinds in a seductive kinetic display of lust owns a brain, and the human brain is the most complex entity in the known universe. The average 'sex tourist' doesn't think about the inner workings of the human body when he is looking for a girl for the night, but I do. As an artist I studied anatomy, so I see a woman's body as a kinetic symphony of bones and muscle, angles, lines of force and mathematical proportions, and Tantra has made me aware of the human body as a miracle of bio-engineering. Sexual objectification becomes a door or magical portal through which I can embrace the wonders of the universe.

Julian Huxley dreamed of a new religion based in science which would have its own rituals and religious architecture. I believe in this also. In Hong Kong there is a beautiful park where the public can practice Tai Chi. There is a Tai Chi garden and an attractive mock Greco-Roman stadium which is also an exercise area. I found these really inspirational when I was in Hong Kong and often practised my martial arts in these beautiful surroundings. I envisage a nationwide infrastructure project that would offer regular work for thousands of artists and craftsman and would be a massive boost for the tourist industry as people from all over the world came to visit the UK as they do for the temples in Thailand. These largely open-air Tantric cathedrals would be the architectural manifestation of a new civic religion of Transhumanism. They would provide alternatives to churches and mosques and would be places for prayer, exercise, dance and meditation as well as funerals, marriages and other civic ceremonies. A transhumanist society would insist on the marginalisation and relegation of all hellfire religion to the status of private faiths, perfunctorily tolerated until they hopefully died out.

But this would only take place of course after a nationwide education programme that would enlighten the public and prepare them for the changes ahead. Hopefully the matter would be settled peacefully and hellfire religionists would recognise they are on the wrong side of history and would be content to take a back seat in the new world order. All faith schools would have to be abolished and a national education system established that taught a transhumanist agenda with a reason-based morality that was infused with the ideals of a rational Godhead, the world citizen, the fellowship of humankind, and a world government.

Prostitution should be encouraged as a social good in a civilized world where anti-erotic superstition would hopefully be a thing of the past. It would naturally involve Tantric principles. Prostitution would be legalised and official areas allocated by the state in major cities as red light districts that would cater both for men and women and would have to meet high aesthetic and spiritual standards. Perhaps brothels should be renamed 'flower houses', and as dens of erotic hedonism they would ideally be sumptuously furnished and adorned with erotic art.

Let us now think outside the box. Lateral thinking is the only way forward. Mary Daly said "If God is male, then male is God". This aphorism implies that men, through patriarchal religion, claim divine authority for themselves, imposing their delusions on all of us. She has exposed the weakness of feminism that seeks to achieve equality in a patriarchal world without realising that as long as the old gods are left intact, this sorry world will remain a doomsday machine, and by gaining short-term success they are perpetuating men's immemorial mistakes and merely feeding the monster. I say "If you get God wrong you get it all wrong". The logic of this is simple: if God is a synonym for truth or ultimate truth, it obviously follows that if you get the core reality of the universe wrong then you are going to get everything else wrong too. If you invent blasphemous fictions at the heart of the universe and then build exclusivist, separatist religions in homage to them, brainwashing billions of people to believe them, you are going to clog up the wheels of progress. We've got God wrong, and Judaism, Christianity and Islam are the main offenders and the principle obstacles to world peace, spiritual unity and progress. It is irrelevant if most Christians and Muslims are good people and some are even active in doing good works; this simply means they are choosing to ignore the dark side of their belief system and living in denial. The only reason Christians do good works is because they believe their religion is true, and they only believe it's true because they are living in denial, so this cycle, this closed circuit thinking, has to be broken. We need to look at what divides us and prevents the necessary advance to a world government and a mono-religious world, and we need to work to remove these divisions. These divisions are caused mainly by nationalism and the cold war mindset, racism, selfish capitalism and hellfire superstition.

In a nutshell, we have a choice between two theoretical 'end time' scenarios. The first end time scenario is a self-fulfilling prophecy inaugurated by religion. The result could be sudden megadeath through nuclear holocaust, or alternatively slow death or degeneration through terminal anarchy and strife due to human failure to deal with mounting problems effectively, especially global warming. To experience this apocalyptic scenario we need do nothing but carry on as we are doing. The second end-time scenario is to save the world by saving God from sado-religion and transplanting God into Transhumanism.

Hence "the end of the world" has two interpretations, namely the literal end of the world perhaps through nuclear war or incremental degeneration, or alternatively the *end of the old world order* dominated by nationalistic politics, selfish capitalism and false religion. Once this is understood the question obviously arises as to how you bring the second and more attractive end time scenario to fruition. Transhumanism is an invitation to atheists, Christians, Muslims and all others to embrace rational religion. Many of us will have to lose God in order to find God.

CHAPTER SEVEN

Amnesty International – the scandal of hypocrisy

The letter below is in response to a letter I wrote to Amnesty International asking them why they did not publically condemn religious doctrines ratifying torture in the next world. It was written by Allan Hogarth, Senior Information Manager, on 30th April 2004.

I put it to them that if their policy is to condemn torture in all circumstances, which is an absolutist position, they should condemn the doctrine of eternal torture in hell because if torture is wrong in this world it must be wrong in the next. Surely the moral condemnation of torture is a categorical imperative and should apply both in secular and religious ethics equally?

I am writing to you regarding the correspondence that you have sent to various people at Amnesty International expressing your concerns about torture and religious doctrine.

As you are no doubt aware, Amnesty International does not take a position on any particular religious conviction. This is precisely because, as you point out, freedom of thought, conscience and religion is a fundamental human right which is enshrined in the Universal Declaration of Human Rights (specifically, Article 18). This includes any ideas which a person may have regarding the afterlife.

The respect and protection of human rights, including the absolute prohibition of torture, does not require changing one's personal religious convictions. Human rights can and should be respected equally by everyone, regardless of one's personal faith or religious views. Responsibility for violations of human rights does not lie with any particular religious beliefs as such, but lies exclusively in the actions of the individual.

Taking a position on specific religious doctrines or beliefs would be a violation of the right to freedom of conscience and religion as well as a violation of the fundamental principle of non-discrimination, which underpins all human rights and guides Amnesty International's work.

I can assure you that Amnesty International condemns in the strongest terms all 'terrorist' attacks, including the attacks of September 11th 2001, but attributes responsibility to the perpetrators on the basis of their actions, as opposed to their particular religious views.

Amnesty International will continue to campaign against torture but will not be publicly condemning any religious doctrines.

I do hope that this letter clarifies Amnesty International's position.

Amnesty's reply to me used a series of arguments that I find wanting. Their first argument is to invoke the Universal Declaration of Human Rights, which enshrines freedom of thought and religion. I am not asking Amnesty to deny the right of religion to teach certain doctrines, merely to offer disapproval in the same way that most of us disapprove of racism and homophobia and torture. So why is Amnesty not willing to exercise its own right to free speech and conscience by passing a broad moral judgement on an evil attitude? It does not have to be accusatory or specific to one particular religion. Most religions have belief in some kind of hell – in fact even Plato, a secular philosopher, makes reference to hell. The law favours protecting religion from hate speech and blasphemy but won't recognise the obvious fact that religion itself can be demonstrated to be blasphemy against God and hate speech against sinners or infidels who are vilified as hell-fodder deserving eternal punishment.

Mr Hogarth then makes the absurd statement that appears to me to say that if you think torture is wrong but your religion condones it, there is no reason to change your religion. This is tantamount to saying that if your religion teaches that racism and paedophilia are virtues you should have no concerns if the secular world regards them as evils. In other words you can have two contradictory ideas of right and wrong – secular morality and religious morality! What then has happened to the Amnesty conviction that the evil of torture is a universal imperative – a moral absolute?

He follows this statement with one that doesn't make a lot of sense to me. It seems to disconnect belief from actions. The belief in hell has been a major force or influence on the actions of believers of all faiths. Saving people from hell has been the main driving force behind Christo-Islamic proselytising over hundreds of years, resulting in brutal conquests, crusades, sectarian wars and horrific violations of human rights. Even today, fear of hell and a longing for paradise and martrydom is the main motivation of Islamic suicide bombers and terrorists. I should also add that what people think, as opposed to what they do, is also well within the moral realm and subject to ethical evaluation. People hold and express all sorts of attitudes that don't necessarily result directly in actions, but they can be very revealing about a person's character. Any attempt to belittle the importance of the 'private' content of the human mind is unrealistic about how humans interrelate and judge each other. The Catholic Church, following the teaching of Jesus, has for centuries made it quite clear that the sinful contents of the mind are just as reprehensible as sinful actions and should be confessed to the priest. Evil thoughts and evil deeds cannot be separated into neatly compartmentalised moral categories.

His next argument is really a rehash of his first argument, and is equally absurd. To express disapproval of the religious doctrine of torture would somehow violate the principle of freedom of religion. The right to freedom of religion does not give believers the right not to be criticised! Then, the excuse that Amnesty cannot discriminate and must be fair to all is invoked to provide justification for not doing the right thing. The point is, Amnesty could condemn religious torture as a generic evil, in the abstract so to speak, attacking a principle without naming and shaming any particular religion – how is this discrimination?

His final concluding statement is a classic exercise in anti-rational doublethink. He cites 9/11/2001. The crime lies in the terrorists' actions and not the religious beliefs that caused it! This is a classic example of how Western civilization will always go to any lengths to divorce religion from evil done in its name. This is a complete denial of the law of cause and effect and is actually completely out of touch with reality and jurisprudence. Many potential terrorists have been jailed for simply plotting to commit acts of terrorism. In these cases no actions were involved - only religious beliefs causing criminal intentions! This is called *mens rea*, which means 'guilty mind'. If the law can send people to prison for a guilty mind, why can't Amnesty come off its self-righteous pedestal and condemn the guilty minds of those who calmly condone the mass infinite torture of their fellow human beings? Amnesty has no credibility, as far as I am concerned, until it does this. The following quotes are taken from a magazine Amnesty produced called *About Amnesty* so that you can judge for yourself whether Amnesty can be accused of a double standard:

We encourage governments, political organisations, businesses, other groups and individuals to support and respect human rights. (P. 2)

Then why not encourage religious organisations to do the same? Why not encourage them to stop attributing sadism to God? Why not encourage them to respect the human rights of the resurrected? Why not encourage them to respect the rights of children to religious self-determination?

We work with trade unions, religious organisations, teachers and other human rights organisation to publicise the Universal Declaration of Human Rights... (P.10)

So when Amnesty are discussing universal human rights

with religious organisations they apparently can't feel any responsibility to raise the issue of supernatural torture and its emphatic inconsistency with Amnesty's own principles. If it's beyond their mandate I say damn their outdated mandate, this is more important! After all, what is their mandate? Is it written in stone? Is it a revelation from God that can't be modified to reflect changing times? Even the American constitution has amendments.

Our members belong to many different faiths. Some governments justify violating human rights by referring to religious teachings. We don't quote these teachings in our appeals, but we do encourage our religious members to use the relevant teachings in their own faith to try to convince other members of their faith to support human rights. (P. 18)

We see from this that Amnesty knows very well that religious ideas can be used to cause human rights abuses but in order to spare religious sensibilities they never mention these ideas. Their silence, like the silence on this matter from society as a whole, is a deliberate and sinister cover-up to hide the most devastating truth of our times, namely that monotheism is causing most of the problems in the world and is arguably out of date, evil, and blasphemous. Amnesty is scared of rocking the boat and offending the great sacred cow whose fake purity has to be protected at any cost. What irony that Christians and Muslims working for Amnesty are by definition completely schizophrenic, on the one hand representing Amnesty, their employer, which condemns torture, and on the other, their religion, which condones it! Amnesty continually justifies its mission with reference to the Universal Declaration of Human Rights. It produced a booklet from which I now quote:

Article 5: No one shall be subjected to torture or to cruel, inhuman or degrading treatment or punishment.

Torture is forbidden at all times and in all circumstances. No one should suffer treatment or punishment that is cruel or makes them feel less than human. These rules apply everywhere – in police stations, prisons, on the streets, in peacetime or during a war.

So we are told these rules apply everywhere, but not apparently in hell! Why is religious morality allowed to exist in its own privileged realm completely exempt from any accountability or responsibility? Why does the religious belief that torture is good and just have the right to exist unchallenged alongside the universal secular belief enshrined in international law that it is the worst crime against humanity? Morality is not, as Amnesty seems to contend, just about actions. It is just as much about what people believe; what they say, what they think and what they write and teach to others.

Article 19: Everyone has the right to freedom of opinion and expression.

You have the right to tell people your opinion. You should be able to express your views, however unpopular, without fear of punishment. You have the right to communicate your views within your country and to people in other countries.

According to Article 19, Amnesty is entitled to express its opinion about the legitimization of mass infinite torture by monotheism, and it refuses to do so, not from any noble ideals, but from cowardice and political correctness. It knows that for Amnesty International, which has a global gravitas, to highlight this scandalous paradox in Western civilization would cause an outcry.

Amnesty has, in theory, the power and influence to oblige the world to completely rethink what we mean by God, religion and religious freedom. To object to terrestrial torture while ignoring and effectively denying the relevance of its supernatural counterpart is to fail to understand they are inseparable and form a seamless reality of moral schizophrenia that warps the soul of the world.

How can Amnesty International continue to ignore the implications of many references to hell in the New Testament and literally hundreds of threats against non-believers in the Koran like the ones quoted below?

Then shall he say also unto them on the left hand, "Depart from me, ye cursed, into everlasting fire prepared for the devil and his angels..." (Matthew 25:41)

But surely, we shall cause those who disbelieve to taste a severe torment, and certainly, We shall requite them the worst of what they used to do. (Surah 41:26)

Those who deny the Book (this Koran)... they will come to know (when they will be cast into the Fire of Hell). When iron collars will be rounded over their necks, and the chains, they shall be dragged along, in boiling water, then they will be burned in the Fire. (Surah 40. 70,71,72)

The tortures in hell, according to the historic teachings of Christians and Muslims, are said to be substantially worse than anything experienced on Earth and sinners and infidels are kept alive and conscious for ever, specifically to be tortured over and over again for all eternity. In an age when Muslim extremists quite regularly murder secular bloggers, artists, writers and film producers for expressing their valid criticisms of Islam, Muslims need to be educated to see that their own religion can be, *by its very existence*, offensive to others. The Bible and the Koran are, in my informed and measured view, actually hate speech against secularists. It is time for non-Muslims to realise this and to let Muslims and Christians know that they don't want to be defined as sinners and infidels deserving punishment, just as black people don't want to be defined as niggers and Jews as Yids. Islamophobia is a monstrous mass media myth. By definition it means an irrational fear of Islam, because a phobia is an irrational fear. But what is the term for its opposite, namely a rational fear of Islam? Why aren't we allowed by the PC media to have a rational aversion to Islam? Islamophobia is a term that when used in today's social context allows no room for a justified rational fear and hatred of Islam. The myth of Islamophobia is uncritically accepted, sustained and nourished by the intelligentsia of the world and is one of the most obscene examples of political correctness that have ever been inflicted on the garrulous public.

Would it really compromise Amnesty International's lofty ideals if it were to make some kind of general declaration without apportioning blame to any particular religion, saying that the ethic of eternal torture in hell espoused by some religious believers is incompatible with the spirit of international law, which declares torture unlawful and morally wrong? They should therefore look to their own conscience as to whether they feel it wise to continue to hold such anti-social and divisive beliefs. Would not such a gentle nudge to the world conscience not be justified, considering the despicable way hell-blindness is completely crippling the global debate about Islamist terrorism? It is hell-blindness that is forcing the debate to go round and round in circles chasing its own tail and endlessly repeating the untruths that Islam is not accountable or responsible for its terrorist offspring and that Islamic extremism can only be defeated through a counter narrative. But this counter-narrative, this antidote to extremism, is never produced. If it is supposed to be a theological explanation as to why extremism is 'wrong', it will never work, in the same way that Catholicism will never trump Protestantism and vice versa. The demonisation of extremists as inhuman, un-Islamic monsters fails to acknowledge their theological legacy, which is very nuanced and complex and can be traced back through a bloody trail to the Muslim Brotherhood.

The only 'counter-narrative' that will work against Islamism is a militant rational assault on Islam itself, because Islam is the root cause of Islamist terrorism. The reason this truth is strenuously resisted by the Christian crusaders, armed to the teeth with their beloved Declaration of Human Rights, is that they know that such an assault on Islam would also be an assault on Christianity. The British establishment bends over backwards to accommodate the cause of so-called moderate Islam in order to protect itself, the monarchy and the Church of England. The British way of life is sustained by a great lie: our national religion which is protected by the blasphemy law is in fact itself a blasphemy! Rule Britannia!

Pagan Tantrism has no hell or Judgement Day. We need a God who de-conflicts the world, which is presently divided by a lethal cocktail of tribal animosities and prejudices based on defective politics and dysfunctional religions. 'God is sex not sadism' is the only zeitgeist that stands any chance of preventing the world from imploding, because the only way of saving the world and ending global corruption, global warming, poverty and war is through synergy and unity and mutual co-operation. We simply must find a better way of working together, and this can only happen if we find a shared, unified Transhumanist morality that is not made totally schizophrenic with gross contradictions from some outdated religious cloud cuckoo land.

How can anyone say that religions with mutually hostile scriptures and widely contradictory definitions of God can ever be a source of meaningful interconnectedness? If diversity is going to work it has to be based on a spiritual commonality – a generic God model that serves as a lingua franca. The present multi-faith principle is a dog's dinner of anti-erotic, anti-life superstitions vying for power and influence in a world already bitterly divided by ethic, tribal and xenophobic borders. Warmongering nationalism and selfish capitalism unite to feed a new arms race and the squandering of trillions of dollars on instruments of death, destruction and torture and all this and much more takes place within the matrix of exponential global warming. Is this not truly a doomsday machine? Who built this machine of megadeath? I contend it was built largely by the archvillains of monotheism: just look at the way Abraham and Moses have come back to life in Israel to do battle with Muhammad. Obama, Putin, Cameron and other world leaders self-identify as Christians. A cartel of Christian crusaders in alliance with other Muslims have declared war on ISIL and the Muslim caliphate. What a mess! Politicians are sometimes well-meaning, intelligent and eloquent, but they are all spiritually retarded, in my view. They are themselves the biggest part of the problems that afflict us. They are failing as our helpers and slowly killing the planet and all hope of progress. They must be seen as our adversaries until they prove themselves to be our guardians. As a species we must re-image God and redefine spiritual enlightenment for our times and make sure we only vote for leaders who conform to this definition, which of course begins with an uncompromising rejection of hellfire religion and therefore a complete reassessment of the shibboleth of blanket religious freedom, devoid of any quality controls.

As my book goes to publication, Syria is boiling over with rage, hate and utterly pointless killing. I have lived on this planet for sixty-nine years waiting for real change, and this is all the world policymakers can offer me and others like me - another demented war where major nations are behaving like irresponsible psychopaths – Olympic champions of collateral damage! All over the world we are murdering millions of innocent children through war and poverty and our failure to cure disease. Do they not deserve better? Are we not supposed to be responsible adults? We need radical change. If you don't like my suggestions, what are yours? Do you have anything as good?

Syria has been turned into an insane geopolitical microcosm of the world, with nations fighting proxy wars in a cesspool of manic violence. While the general population is being decimated, or forced to migrate to refugee camps, tribal, sectarian and international coalitions are all vying for power and influence. You couldn't find a better example of Christian crusaders and Muslim extremists creating hell on earth than this. With NATO, Russia and others locked into this nightmare scenario, there is a real risk of fatal escalation. Turkey, a Muslim country, is tragically a member of NATO and is in a serious diplomatic spat with Russia, and both are meddling in Syria with opposite agendas that could suck us all into a global conflict. As a pagan watching from the sidelines I'm sure of one thing – I don't want to die for Islam. Islam is not worth dying for or killing for – in fact Islam is not even worth believing in. We've come full circle in my lifetime – we are almost back at the Cuban Missile Crisis - only now with religious madness rampaging across the planet its actually got far worse! This crisis, no doubt, will be resolved in some way with luck, but others will follow until the end time when our luck finally runs out.

God does not torture his creatures in hell. God is sex. God is men and women making love and experiencing the greatest joy of life whether it's in prostitution or marriage, whether it's for procreation, or recreation. Make love not war, or better still, make Tantric love not war. Our news reports detail the daily carnage when the sacred bodies given to us by God are disgustingly mutilated in torture, blown to pieces by bombs, burned and desecrated with chemical weapons and shot with guns. Tantra teaches respect for the human body as God's masterpiece. Tantra celebrates life and joy. Transhumanism calls for men and women to work together and share the planet's resources so that as artists of life we can make our own masterpiece – a civilised world where there is no need for poverty or national borders. Imagine a world, said John Lennon, with no religion or nations and no heaven and hell. Imagine it and make it happen through Tantra!

God is sex, not sadism. Sex is the great equaliser, and it doesn't care about ethnic or national borders or divisions. The hearts, minds and sexual organs of lovers will find each other, come what may, through any artificial barriers. Falling in love is the most beautiful human experience. Let us fall in love with peace and harmony and the world citizen and the world federation where diversity can flourish but like different coloured beads on the same thread of pure gold – the 'It' God – the great ineffable power at the heart of the universe that does not write silly books or torture fornicators.

Identify the big picture! We are now in the foothills of Armageddon, but there are two Armageddons and we have a choice. We have a choice to go on or change direction. If we stay on this road the world will simply get worse, because the doomsday machine will have no choice but to follow its religious programming. If we choose change we have to stop being super-nice, over-tolerant people and become spiritual warriors and militant rationalists who will no longer indulge the evil fantasies of those who have stolen the planet from us and poisoned its wells and made deserts of its pastures. The new world order will not come without a mighty fight, and as Bertrand Russell said, the adversary is not going to lie down and say die. Because monotheism is anti-rational and based in the epistemology of blind faith, rationalism will only be partially effective. To win the intellectual battle is the easy part but to make it stick, to make it dent the armour plating of the beast, may take a few big thumps from a very big club. This is the final battle – the apocalyptic end time when rationalism has to prove itself against a worthy enemy - and when rationalism finally emerges the victor, it will be battle-hardened and honed to perfection and ready to rebuild civilization and the new world order – maybe not paradise on Earth, but close.

However, monotheism over the centuries has built prodigious defences against rationalism, which is why reason can't do the job by itself. It needs help from something madly, insanely impactful and attention-grabbing that will ignite mass media on a global scale and galvanise a concurrent awakening of militant rationalism - we need, as I have suggested before, some wild maenad women dancing outside holy buildings and demanding the demise of the male gods of violence and torture. Pussy Riot, the punk band that staged a protest in a Moscow church in 2012 had to take a serious hit in Putin's Russia. Their protest however, fell short of an ideological attack on Christianity. Unfortunately, it wasn't aimed at doctrine or dogma but the support the Russian Orthodox Church gave to Putin. The way they were shut down is an indication of how much guts and dedication protesters would need, but is that too much to ask for saving the world from false prophets - the superbugs?

Such political activism using one of women's most powerful devices, namely guerrilla dance, is difficult to clearly envisage and would probably be very limited for obvious reasons in most Muslim countries. It would however certainly work in America and Europe. The Vatican, as the perfect instantiation of male privilege, undeserved political influence and sadomythic superstition, should be the principle target for such a movement.

Conclusion

My paintings are a summons to revolution and spiritual renewal. They are a political manifesto. They are not like any artwork that has existed before. They are mandalas and they are political posters and they are Aquarian testaments. They celebrate, nudism, dance, the human body, sexual love, women's spiritual liberation, prostitution and pagan transhumanism. They call for a new world order based on the ideal of the world citizen who takes pride in simply being a human being irrespective of blood or nation. My erotic images are overlaid with religio-political slogans or aphorisms that ensure that the viewer/reader has no doubts about what the imagery is intended to mean for the artist. Accordingly images of naked sex workers have radical seditious aphorisms superimposed over them. The erotic images themselves symbolise the metaphysical pleasure principle of Tantra which explains why I use images of naked girls as a vehicle for promulgating the wider principle that sex is the life force and God is sex. The maxims represent Tantra's iconoclastic and transgressive contempt for authority and convention. All but two of the following examples are my own original mantras which I reproduce on my images:

If you get God wrong, you get it all wrong.

Make love not war.

I just want to fuck women – I don't want to burn them in hell.

If torture is wrong in this world, it's wrong in the next.

Why call us criminals – I need her and she needs my money?

God is sex – not sadism.

If God is male, then male is God.

It takes evolution to make men out of monkeys but it takes religion to make monkeys out of men.

We are one family – we are world citizens, so leave your tribe.

Politicians are metaphysical morons.

God does not write books.

Feminists against men who need prostitutes and strippers are bimbos with Stockholm syndrome.

Don't ask if God is true – ask if religion is true to God.

Go pagan, but if you don't we won't send you to hell.

Amnesty International condemns torture in this world but not in the next. Why not?

Women will only be liberated when they liberate both themselves and God from patriarchal sadoreligion.

Men who claim to know the mind of God know nothing but their own conceit.

Theology is monkey babble discussing fictional bananas.

Religious freedom is a fine principle but which religions are worthy of it?

Blasphemies masquerading as religions are a cancer in the world soul.

Nationalism in the 21ˢᵗ century is xenophobia and an insult to world citizenship.

Sex workers of the world unite against Jesus and Muhammad – your worst critics.

Tantric sex is self-empowerment – Tantric sex is a martial art.

If the Christian Church is good, how come it murdered 100 million American pagans with the help of God-sent smallpox and scripture?

If Islam is a religion of peace, how come it terrorized India for centuries, slaughtered 300 million Hindu pagans and demolished thousands of temples?

In Tantra, nudism, prostitution and fornication are sacraments, not sins.

A phobia is an irrational fear. If Islamophobia is an irrational fear of Islam, what is the word for a rational *fear of Islam?*

Because the supremacy of rationalism over blind faith is never required as a pre-condition for democracy, it is always in danger from creeping theocracy.

Islamophobia is a myth - to fear Islam is not a phobia but an obligation.

It's a myth that all religions are just different paths to the same God. Most religions are dead ends or worse.

Charity has a dark side – it covers up the failure of politicians to deliver a world where it is not needed.

Men are natural voyeurs and viewers of feminine nudity, for which they are chastised by those who fail to to share their passion for God's masterpiece.

Men who love the beauty of nature are called poets, but men who love the beauty of naked women are called lechers.

The male gaze is only stigmatised because women have failed to develop their own.

Atheism only makes matters worse – by failing to prove God doesn't exist it gives the follies of faith a stay of execution.

Atheists have lost the plot – to believe in God is not irrational but to believe in an irrational God surely is.

Tantric sex is sedition .

Jesus Christ – sadist or saviour?

Hitler only wanted to exterminate the Jews – Jesus wants to keep them alive forever to suffer torture.

Monotheism is blasphemy – this is help speech not hate speech.

By hating sado-religion you are loving truth.

Don't bother to vote – what is the point of voting for your executioners?

Politicians are the problem, so how can problems solve problems?

Since most religion is anti-erotic, religious freedom means war on sex.

Space exploration is a waste of time if Jesus is coming back.

What is the sound of one hand clapping? Who gives a fuck? – Zen Buddhism can't change the world, but Tantric Buddhism can!

Tantric Humanism – the solution.

If religion recommended paedophilia we wouldn't tolerate it, so why do we tolerate religion that sanctifies torture?

Accusing hell believers of being retarded is not hate speech – it's shock therapy.

Islamic terrorism is a monster created by Islam, Christian crusaders and the failure of feminism to identify the enemy.

The problem that faces humanity is not proving the existence of God but proving the truth of religion.

Men who take photographs of stars are called astronomers, but those who take photos of starbursts are called perverts.

The world is a madhouse made in the image of monotheism.

The test of true religion is whether it can save us in this world, not the next.

The Koran teaches Allah's mercy – burn women in hell! The Bible teaches God's love – burn women in hell!

Jesus the arsonist – Muhammad the pyromaniac.

Yoni puja – ban the burka.

You don't need books and prophets to find God – all you need is wonderlust for the universe.

The stripper only reveals the summit of visual experience, and for this she is stigmatised

What does the Burka tell us about a woman? It tells us she is anonymous and deleted. Surely it's better to be a sex object than nothing?

The cause of terrorism is radicalisation – the cure for radicalisation is apostasy.

There are many names for the vagina but the best by far is the Holy Grail.

If we are denied the right to tell Muslims the truth about their religion, they will continue to believe its falsehoods.

The male gaze is the third eye of Tantric wisdom - it sees the path to God through sex.

Moses, Jesus and Muhammad – the superbugs.

Feminists call the male gaze 'sexual objectification'; Muslims call it 'fornication of the eyes' ; Christians call it 'adultery of the heart'; Pagans call it 'a mental hard-on'.

Religious freedom without quality controls is a licence for child abuse.

Women's equality's a joke until they get rid of the Pope.

The Devil's Wager – can you beat it?

Christians have always accused science of their own crime, namely playing God.

The love of freedom without the love of truth is a recipe for anarchy.

If you are right then every time someone attacks you, you grow stronger, because your attackers at best will only be half right.

Nudism won't work on public transport or in the workplace, but what's wrong with the beach?

What's wrong with schoolchildren being shown nude dance or naked yoga? They deserve something better than the censored body.

Nature did not make the human body with no-go zones that have to be shamefully hidden. The body can only be correctly understood as a holistic system of equal components.

It is vital to understand that to terminate hellfire superstition is not a violation of religious freedom or an aspersion against God. Both belief in God and religious freedom would be greatly enhanced by removing monotheism. If we are serious about defending this principle of religious tolerance we need to be sure it is not abused by allowing its blessing to be granted to any cult or superstition that is radically opposed to scientific truth and to values that we can be sure are true. It is never right to sacrifice truth to freedom. Both are equally important. Beliefs cannot be true simply because faith says they are. Only reason has the right to vet and veto cults in order to protect children and society from extreme follies entering the mainstream culture. Secular morals themselves are always evolving, but there are some constants that religion cannot be allowed to challenge. Such a secular moral absolute - an eternal universal truth – a categorical imperative - is that torture is wrong and the eternal gratuitous torture of 'unbelievers' is infinitely wrong.

It may be true in extreme cases that torture could be justified to extract life-saving information, although this theory is rejected by many experts, but torture as a punishment that is not corrective or reformative and lasts for some time, perhaps eternity, is an absolute evil. It must also be understood that many of the hellfire preachers and protagonists of Christian theology have proposed that the tortures in hell are unimaginably worse than anything that can be experienced on Earth and that the 'abominable fancy' is morally justified. St Augustine believed in the abominable fancy, which declares that the saved in heaven will be able to gloat and rejoice over the agony of the damned from a vantage point in heaven from which all of hell will be made visible to them. This is to say nothing of the damnation and torture of unbaptized babies that has been a hallowed belief of many Christians down the centuries. Tantric Humanism and its pleasure principle is diametrically opposed to monotheism with its sadomythic torture ethic. Life is about joy, and if punishment exists in the afterlife it would have to be proportionate, educational and consistent with divine love.

Religions that stand in direct opposition to scientific truth and a proven moral absolute are unworthy of the principle of religious freedom. They have no right to the protection of this noble ideal we all believe in. Religious freedom should not be used and abused to rubber-stamp proven blasphemies. We only show respect for the freedom principle by making sure its hallowed integrity is not compromised by forcing it to sanction evil and blasphemy defined by reason not faith. The question that should concern modern civilization is not whether God is true or not but whether religion is true to God!

If the reader is still not convinced that we need to review our assessment of monotheism, let me quote Richard Dawkins, who made a startling accusation in *The God Delusion:*

The God of the Old Testament is arguably the most unpleasant character in all fiction: jealous and proud of it; a vindictive, bloodthirsty ethnic cleanser; a misogynistic, homophobic, racist, infanticidal, genocidal, filicidal, pestilential, megalomaniacal, sadomasochistic, capriciously malevolent bully. (P 51)

Although Dawkins would never be so temeritous as to admit it, the accurate description he offers us of Yahweh would also fit very well with Hitler. On the basis of this character assassination by Dawkins (and many other academics before him) is it not justifiable to ask the question seriously whether religious Jews worship Hitler writ large in the sky? Is this not the ultimate irony? Only religion could produce something as grotesquely insane as

Jews worshipping a cosmic Hitler!

But Dawkins makes a fatal error when he falls into the common trap of thinking Jesus is an improvement on Yahweh:

Well, there's no denying that, from a moral point of view, Jesus is a huge improvement over the cruel ogre of the Old Testament. Indeed Jesus, if he existed (or whoever wrote his script if he didn't) was surely one of the great ethical innovators of history. (P.283)

I don't know if Dawkins has seen the fatal error in his thinking since writing *The God Delusion*, because in the same book he expresses his abhorrence of hellfire but seemingly fails to link it to Jesus. If Yahweh is Hitler then Jesus, as I have already demonstrated, is worse than Hitler and Muhammad logically must be worse than either of them, because the Koran teaches hellfire even more emphatically than the New Testament. But the media, academia and world leaders continue to parrot the same old mental habits that regard the default definition of monotheism as the moral bedrock of Western civilization. This is the nature of the madhouse we now live in – the doomsday machine set up by Abraham, Moses, Jesus and Muhammad and sustained and protected by political correctness and hell-blindness.

Postscript

Every year many countries celebrate The Holocaust Remembrance Day. The same thing cannot be said of the two pagan holocausts by Christians and Muslims, which make the Nazis look like daisy pickers.

Might I suggest to pagans in Britain that they stop being so PC and polite about Christianity and Islam – their ideological and historical adversaries. A first step towards re-launching paganism in the 21st century would be a pagan Holocaust Remembrance Day to honour the millions of pagans tortured to death in the Americas by Christian fanatics and the millions of Hindu polytheists decimated by Muslim barbarians practising their 'religion of peace'. The Hindu holocaust has been called the worst genocide in history: it is undoubtedly the worst mass killing of pagans and emphatically refutes any claims by Muslims that Islam is a religion of peace. The world needs to be reminded that the dark historic crimes of Christianity and Islam are repeated by Islam via ISIL today and are ingenuously called non-Islamic!

Politicians are tasked with being artists and creators. The world is their canvas and their calling is to paint a beautiful picture of sunny paradise. The world should be full of joy and celebration and instead it is a madhouse teetering on a cliff edge. Instead of utopia we have dystopia, run by little Hitlers playing their selfish Machiavellian power games. They don't care about us or anybody or anything except their own thirst for power and wealth. Self-preservation is their only concern and to this they sacrifice everything and everybody. Syria now in meltdown is a microcosm of the world today and exemplifies everything that's wrong with politicians. Why do they never heed the simple wisdom of John Lennon.

John Lennon sings his wisdom from the grave. He serenades the dictators with his dulcet tones of wisdom that fall on deaf ears. Like Julian Huxley, like Bertrand Russell, like Mary Daly, Lennon tells the hell believers and the hell makers how to change course and to start making heaven on Earth. We have to make them listen! We have to tell these warmongering dinosaurs that God is sex, not sadism.

IMAGINE

John Lennon

Imagine there's no heaven
It's easy if you try
No hell below us
Above us only sky
Imagine there's no countries
It isn't hard to do
Nothing to kill or die for
And no religion too
Imagine all the people
Living life in peace

You may say I'm a dreamer
But I'm not the only one
I hope someday you'll join us
And the world will be as one

Imagine no possessions
I wonder if you can
No need for greed or hunger
A brotherhood of man
Imagine all the people
Sharing all the world

You may say I'm a dreamer
But I'm not the only one
I hope someday you'll join us
And the world will live as one.

www.ingramcontent.com/pod-product-compliance
Lightning Source LLC
La Vergne TN
LVHW051255080426
835509LV00020B/2990